UG KRISHNAMURTI

UNPLUGGED

UG KRISHNAMURTI UNPLUGGED

On Certainty, Love, Society and Truth

SUNITA PANT BANSAL

Foreword by
MAHESH BHATT

MOTILAL BANARSIDASS INTERNATIONAL DELHI

First Edition: Delhi, 2023

ISBN : 978-81-19394-14-2

Also available at
MOTILAL BANARSIDASS INTERNATIONAL
H. O. : 41 U.A. Bungalow Road, (Back Lane) Jawahar Nagar, Delhi - 110 007
4261/3 (basement), Ansari Road, Darya Ganj, New Delhi - 110 002
203 Royapettah High Road, Mylapore, Chennai - 600 004
12/1A, 2nd Floor, Bankim Chatterjee Street, Kolkata - 700 073
Stockist : Motilal Books, Ashok Rajpath, Near Kali Mandir, Patna - 800 004

Printed in India
MOTILAL BANARSIDASS INTERNATIONAL

PREFACE

I chanced upon UG's books as a fledgling publisher and with Mahesh Bhatt's encouragement, gave them a new look and launched them in the market. A decade later, I reviewed them and felt that they needed complete rehauling and revamping.

Meanwhile, I had met not only UG but also many of his friends and followers. I found that a number of people 'felt' UG but could not quite comprehend the 'feeling'. They read his words, but somehow could not quite 'read' them. I wondered why... till one particular person said that his books have far too much stuff! There is a lot of jumping in the discussions, from one topic to another – creating confusion. That hit the bull's eye for me!

Now I had a mission... I sat down with all the material that I had. I did not see them as independent books, but as a huge sea of words. I read everything and made different topics under which I could put down UG's words. The various topics that emerged from this churning of words were: reality, truth, love, body, death, society, certainty, understanding and so on. The logical step forward was to slot the material under these themes.

The result is there for all to see.

These are UG's words... undiluted, uninterrupted...

Enjoy!

Sunita Pant Bansal

FOREWORD

The Aftertaste

No story has a beginning or an end. Arbitrarily one chooses that moment of experience from which to look back or from which to look ahead. The aftertaste of my address at the International Conference of Spirituality, which was held at the School of Management Sciences, Varanasi, left me with a deepening feeling that the human race is not ready to let go of its fairy tales in its quest for permanence. I guess it's tough for people to accept that the tragedy of the human race springs from its constant desire for an illusion of something that endures, like the soul, an afterlife, and a heaven with God within.

"What did you make of my rantings?" I asked one of the delegates from the Jewish faith, after I had given my talk there. I had run into her in the lift of my hotel, on the night before my departure back to Mumbai from Varanasi. She stared at me as if trying to figure me out. The dying embers of my speech were perhaps glowing somewhere in the depths of her mind. "It undermines everything that we were talking about for the last two days in this convention," she said slowly, as if searching for some answers.

"That's good," I said. "What I really came to share in this seminar were the gropings of my spiritual journey, and the frustration of not being able to sum up anything for certainty. The holy grail for me, if there is one, is the image of my friend, philosopher and guide, the most subversive man to have walked on this planet, UG Krishnamurti... looking at life in his sunset hours with the expression of a child in his crib looking at the world for the first time."

I could see that this woman had not come to this country, the land of the sages and seers, and to a city where the Buddha had given his first discourse, only to be told that the spiritual treasure that the human race keeps talking about does not exist. She was not ready for that. And nor is the world for that matter.

As I took off for Mumbai, I couldn't help marvelling at the guts of the organisers of this unusual institution to have invited a person like me and allowed me to make my iconoclastic address, the theme of which was ironically called 'Icon'. But then I realised, that was the glory of true Hindu thought. It breeds and lives on the idea of *neti neti*, which means 'continuous rejection.'

As the head of the institution summed up my address to one of the faculty members later, "true spirituality is not following, but rejecting". "Mr. Mahesh Bhatt, in fact, is a true Hindu at heart," he said.

The next day, I was amused to learn that a lady delegate from the United States of America, which is perceived to consist of people who are more 'evolved' than those in the third world, had refused to accept my book A *Taste of Life*, (which chronicles the last days of UG Krishnamurti and in a way is the essence of my world view and who I am); saying that she didn't want to have anything to do with the works of such a man, who had debunked the idea of resurrection! All I had said was that if the narrative of Jesus had ended with the crucifixion of Christ, and with him uttering 'Oh lord why hath thou forsaken me,' it wouldn't be the multibillion dollar industry that it is today. I had backed up this utterance of mine on the podium by giving a vivid description of the image of UG Krishnamurti breathing his last in the glory of the morning light with a million ants about to devour a part of his face. This was resurrection – when the dying form of UG was lending itself to the ants as food and nourishment and contributing to the continuity of life.

That was eternity in a moment. Where the subject (in whatever form) exists in order that 'life' (in whatever form) may continue.

It was thus so fitting that, that was exactly what I had seen on the banks of the Ganga, the previous evening. As the sun set, corpses were being burned, and the fire from the pyres was merging with the orange of the setting sun. At the same time, the ashes from the bodies already burned, became a part of the mighty Ganga, which kept flowing; and alongside all this drama of death, life went on relentlessly; the children played cricket, and the temple bells were ringing out. Life and death were co-existing there on the banks of the Ganges, as they have done for centuries, and will continue to do so for centuries to come. I guess this luminous moment of understanding could only come to me in Kashi, whose name itself denotes light.

I only hope that those who view my utterances as anti-Christian, or anti God, give their heart to these words from the Bible... 'The light shineth in the darkness, but the darkness comprehendeth not.'

But, as I said from the podium, in the conclusion of my heartfelt address, whatever I have spoken is my lyric and my song. I have no wish to impose this on anyone as a national anthem or a global anthem. Because what resonated in my heart when I went to Sarnath, the place where the Buddha gave his first discourse after enlightenment, and where the Buddhist sangha came into existence was this: that by introducing proselytization or conversion into human thought, the sage had unwittingly given birth to a common mould through which it hoped to manufacture clones. That is why, 2500 years later, what we have created are just imitators, and not another Buddha. When will we learn that you cannot manufacture a sage on an assembly line, through universities or sanghas? They are the gift of life to life.

UG was one such gift.

Mahesh Bhatt

Contents

1.

CERTAINTY

Life has no beginning, no end...

The Certainty That Blasts Everything

The peace you are seeking is already inside you, in the harmonious functioning of the body.

I can never sit on a platform and talk. It is too artificial. It is a waste of time to sit and discuss things in hypothetical or abstract terms. An angry man does not sit and talk and converse pleasantly about anger; he is too angry. So don't tell me that you are in crisis, that you are angry. Why talk of anger? You live and die in the hope that someday, somehow, you will no longer be angry. You are burdened with hope, and if this life seems hopeless, you invent the next life. There are no lives to come.

You come; I talk. What am I to do? Do you want me to criticize you? It is useless, for you are affected by nothing. Having erected impenetrable armour around yourself, you feel nothing. Unable to understand your situation, you react through thoughts, which are your ideas and mentations. Reaction is thought.

The pain you are going through there is clearly reflected without having to experience the pain here. Here there is no experience at all. That is all. In this natural state you feel the pain of others, whether you personally know them or not. Recently my eldest son was dying of cancer in a hospital nearby. I was in the area and visited him often. Friends said that I was in intense pain during the whole time, until he died. I cannot do anything. It (pain) is an expression of life. They wanted me to attempt some kind of healing for his cancer. If I touch that tumour it will grow, for I am adding life to it. Cancer is a multiplication of cells; another expression of life, and anything I might do only strengthens it.

Suffering is an experience, and there is no experience here. You are not one thing, and life another. It is one unitary movement and anything I say about it is misleading, confusing. You are not a 'person', not a 'thing', not a discreet entity surrounded by 'other' things. The unitary movement is not something that you can experience.

What I am saying conflicts with your logical framework. You are using logic to continue that separative structure, that is all. Your questions are again thoughts and therefore reactive. All thought is reactive. You are desperately protecting this armour, this shield of thought, and are frightened that the movement of life might smash your frontiers. Life is like a river in spate, lashing at the banks, threatening the limits that have been placed around it. Your thought structure and your actual physiological framework are limited, but life itself is not. That is why life in freedom is painful to the body; the tremendous outburst of energy that takes place here is a painful thing to the body, blasting every cell as it goes. You cannot imagine how it is in your wildest dreams. This is why it is misleading no matter how I put it.

For you, it is just words; your belief in a unitary movement of life is just a groundless belief, lacking any certainty. You have cleverly rationalized what the gurus and holy books have taught you. Your beliefs are the result of blind acceptance of authority, all second-hand stuff. You are not separate from your beliefs. When your precious beliefs and illusions come to an end, you come to an end. My talking is nothing more than a response to your pain, which you are expressing through questions, logical arguments, and other mentations.

There is nobody here talking, giving advice, feeling pain, or experiencing anything at all. Like a ball thrown against the wall, it bounces back, that is all. My talking is the direct result of your questions, I have nothing here of my own, no obvious or hidden agenda, no product to sell, no axe to grind, nothing to prove.

It is the body that is immortal. It only changes its form after clinical death, remaining within the flow of life in new shapes. The body is not concerned with 'the afterlife' or any kind of permanency. It struggles to survive and multiply now. The fictitious 'beyond', created by thought out of fear, is really the demand for more of the same, in modified form. This demand for repetition of the same thing over and over again is the demand for permanence. Such permanence is foreign to the body. Thought's demand for permanence is choking the body and distorting perception. Thought sees itself as not just the protector of its own continuity, but also the body's continuity. Both are utterly false.

If some sort of radical change occurs through no volition of yours, then that is the end of it. You will have no way of stopping it, of changing the situation at all. You cannot but go through it. It does no good to question reality. Question, rather, your goals, your beliefs, and assumptions. It is from them, not reality, that you must be freed. These pointless questions you are asking will disappear with the automatic abandonment of your goals. They are interdependent. One can't exist without the other.

If you drown, you drown. But what good are my assurances to you? Worthless, I'm afraid. You will continue doing what you are doing; its meaninglessness does not even occur to you. I tell you, when you stop doing things out of hope and the desire for continuity, all you do along with it stops. You will stay afloat. But still the hope remains there, "There must be *some* way… perhaps I am not doing it the right way…" In other words, we have to accept the absurdity of depending upon *anything*. We must face our helplessness.

Your problems continue because of the false solutions you have invented. If the answers are not there, the questions cannot be there. They are interdependent; your problems and solutions go together. Because you want to use certain answers to end your problems, those problems, continue. The numerous solutions offered by all these holy people, the psychologists, the politicians, are not really solutions at all. That is obvious. If there were legitimate answers, there would be no problems. They can only exhort you to try harder, practise more meditations, cultivate humility, stand on your head, and more and more of the same. That is all they can do. The teacher, guru, or leader who offers solutions is also false, along with his so-called answers. He is not doing any honest work, only selling a cheap, shoddy commodity in the marketplace. If you brushed aside your hope, fear, and naiveté and treated these fellows like a businessman, you would see that they do not deliver the goods, and never will. But you go on and on buying these bogus wares offered by the so-called experts.

All their philosophies cannot compare to the native wisdom of the body itself. What they are calling mental activity, spiritual activity, emotional activity, and feelings are really all one unitary process. This body is highly intelligent and does not need these scientific or theological teachings to survive and procreate. Take away all your fancies about life, death, and freedom, and the body remains unscathed, functioning harmoniously. It does not need your or my help. You don't have to do a thing. You will never again ask stupid, idiotic questions about immortality, afterlives, or death. The body is immortal.

If you commit suicide, it does not help the situation in any way. The moment after suicide the body begins to decay, returning back to other, differently organized forms of life. When you die, you are adding to the continuity of life, putting an end to nothing. *Life has no beginning and no end.* A dead and dying body feeds the hungry ants there in the grave, and rotting corpses give off soil-enriching chemicals, which in turn nourish other life forms. You cannot put an end to your life; it is impossible.

The body is mortal and never asks silly questions like, "Is there immortality?" It knows that it will come to an end in that particular form, only to continue on in others. Questions about life after death are always asked out of fear.

Those people who direct your 'spiritual life' cannot be honest about these things, for they make a living out of fear, speculations about future life, and the 'mystery' of death.

And as for you, you are not really interested in the future of man, only your own petty little destinies. It is just a ritual you go through, talking for hours and hours about mankind, compassion, and the rest. It is you that you are interested in, otherwise there would not be this childish interest in your future lives, and your imminent demise.

You are all neurotic people. You talk against birth control, drone on and on about the preciousness of life, then bomb and massacre! It is too absurd. You are concerned with an unborn life while you are killing thousands and thousands of people by bombing, starvation, poverty, and terrorism. Your 'concern' about life is only to make a political issue out of it. It is just an academic discussion. I am not interested in that.

Are you really interested? Are you interested in the future of mankind? Your expressions of anger, righteousness, and caring have no meaning for me. It is just a ritual. You sit and talk, that's all. You are not at all angry. If you were angry at this moment, you would not ask this question, even to yourself. You sit everlastingly talking of anger. The angry wouldn't talk about it. The body has already reacted with regard to that anger by absorbing it. The anger is burnt, finished then and there. You don't do anything; the body just absorbs it. That is all. If all this is too much for you, if it depresses you, don't ever go to the holy men. Take pills, do anything, but don't expect the holy business to help you. It is a waste of time.

As long as you think you have something to renounce, you are lost. Not to think of money and the necessities of life, is an illness. It is a perversion to deny yourself the basic needs of life.

You think that through a self-imposed asceticism you will increase your awareness and then be able to use that awareness to be happy. No chance. You will be peaceful when all your ideas about awareness are dropped and you begin to function like a computer. You must be a machine, function automatically in this world, never questioning your actions before, during, or after they occur.

All moral, spiritual, ethical values are false. The psychologists, searching for a pragmatic way out, are now at the end of their tethers, even turning to the spiritual people for answers. They are lost, and yet the answers must come from them, not from the encrusted, useless traditions of holy business.

The so-called messiahs have left nothing but misery in this world. If a modern messiah came before you, he would be unable to help you at all. And if he can't help, no one can.

Truth is a movement. You can't capture it, contain it, give expression to it, or use it to advance your interests. The moment you capture it, it ceases to be truth. What is the truth for me is something that cannot, under any circumstances be communicated to you. The certainty here cannot be transmitted to another. For this reason, the whole *guru* business is absolute nonsense. This has always been the case, not just now. Your self-denial is to enrich the priests. You deny yourself your basic needs while that man travels in a Rolls Royce car, eating like a king, and being treated like a potentate. He, and the others in the holy business, thrive on the stupidity and credulity of others. The politicians, similarly, thrive on the gullibility of man. It is the same everywhere.

Doing away with the gurus, temples, and holy books as a prescription for freedom is ridiculous. You search for answers only as remedies for your problems, to avoid pain. But life is nothing but pain. Your birth is pain. Everything that is born is painful. There is no use asking why it is so. It is so. You think that by renouncing *gurus* and authorities you will suffer some divine endurance;

endurance of pain is not going to help you spiritually. There is no way.

There is a solution for your problem – death. That freedom you are interested in can come about only at the point of death. Everybody attains *moksha* eventually, for, *moksha* always foreshadows death, and everyone dies.

When you die the body is in a prostrate position, it stops functioning, and that is the end of it. But in this case the body somehow renewed itself. It happens daily as a matter of course now; the whole process took years to stabilize. For me life and death are one, not two separate things. Just let me warn you that if what you are aiming at – *moksha* – really happens, you will die. There will be a physical death, because there has to be a physical death to be in that state. It is like playing around with controlling your breath because you find it amusing. But if you hold the breath long enough, you choke to death.

To describe that state as a meditative state full of awareness is romantic hogwash. Awareness! What a fantastic gimmick used to fool themselves and others. You can't be aware of every step; you only become self-conscious and awkward if you do. I once knew a man who was a harbour pilot. He had been reading about 'passive awareness' and attempted to put it into practice. He, for the first time, nearly wrecked the ship he was guiding. Walking is automatic, and if you try to be aware of every step, you will go crazy. So don't invent meditative steps. Things are bad enough. The meditative state is worse.

I don't believe in education. You can teach a technique – mathematics, auto mechanics – but not integrity. How can you teach them about non-greed and non-ambition in an insanely greedy and ambitious society? You will only succeed in making them more neurotic.

Your religious ambitions are just like the businessman's there. If you can't cheat there is something wrong. How do you think the rich man there got his great wealth? Through lectures about non-greed and selflessness? Not at all. He got it by cheating somebody. Society, which is immoral to begin with, says that cheating is immoral, and that non-cheating is moral. I don't see the difference. If you get caught, they put you in jail. So, your food and shelter are provided for. Why worry? It is the guilt you have that compels you to talk of non-greed while you continue on with your greedy life. Your non-greed is invented by thought to keep you from facing the fact that greed is all that is there. But you are not satisfied with what is so. If there were nothing more than that, what would you do? That is all that is there. You just have to live with it. You can't escape. All thought can do is repeat itself over and over again. That is all it can do. And anything repetitive is senile.

If your meditation, *sadhana*, methods and techniques meant anything, you wouldn't be here asking these questions. They are all means for you to bring about change. I maintain that there is nothing to change or transform. You accept that there is something to change as an article of faith. You never question the existence of the one who is to be changed. The whole mystique of enlightenment is based upon the idea of transforming yourself. I cannot convey or transmit my certainty that you and all the authorities down through the centuries are false. They and the spiritual goods they peddle are utterly false. Because I cannot communicate this certainty to you, it would be useless and artificial for me to get up on a platform and hold it forth. I prefer to talk informally. I just say, 'Nice meeting you'.

There is no particular charm is being antisocial. I don't give people what they want. When they realize they will not get what they want here, they invariably go away. As they are leaving for the last time, I like to add the rider, "You won't get it anywhere."

When people come to talk, they find themselves confronted with silence itself. That is why everybody who comes is automatically silent thereafter. If he cannot stand the silence and insists upon talking and discussing things, he will be forced to disagree and walk out. But if you stay long, you will be silenced, not because it is over persuasive, more rational than you are, but because it is silence itself silencing that movement there.

That silence burns everything here. All experiences are burnt. That is why talking to people doesn't exhaust me. It is energy to me that is why I can talk for the whole day without showing any fatigue. Talking with so many people over the years has had no impact upon me. All that they or I have said is burnt here, leaving no trace. This is not, unfortunately, the case with you.

Accepting the limitation is intelligence. You are trying to free yourself from these natural limitations and that is the cause of your sorrow and pain. Your actions are such that one action limits the next action. Your action at this moment is limiting the next action. This action is a reaction. The question of freedom of action does not even arise. Therefore, no fatalistic philosophy is needed. The word *karma* means an action without a reaction. Any action of yours limits the action that is to take place next.

Any action that takes place at the conscious level of your thinking existence is a reaction. Pure, spontaneous action free of all previous actions is meaningless. The one and only action is the response of this living organism to the stimuli around it. That stimulus-response process is a unitary phenomenon. There is no division between action and reaction except when thought interferes and artificially separates them. Otherwise, it is an automatic, unitary process and there is nothing you can do to stop it. There is no need to stop it.

Just as in reality there is no separation of action and reaction, so there is no room for the religious man in the natural scheme of things. The fresh movement of life threatens his source of power and prestige. Still, he does not want to retire. He must be thrown out. Religion is not a contractual arrangement, either public or private. It has nothing to do with the social structure or its management. Religious authority wants to continue its hold on the people, but religion is entirely an individual affair. The saints and saviours have only succeeded in setting you adrift in life with pain and misery and the restless felling that there must be something more meaningful or interesting to do with one's life.

Existence is all that is important, not how to live. We have created the 'how' to live, which in turn has created this dilemma for us. Your thinking has created this dilemma for us. Your thinking has created problems – what to eat, to wear, how to behave –the body doesn't care. I am simply pointing out the absurdity of this conversation. Once you get the hang of it, you just go. I have no message to give mankind.

We have set in motion irreversible forces. We have polluted the sky, the waters, everything. Nature's laws know no reward. Only punishment. The reward is only that you are in harmony with nature. The whole problem started when man decided that the whole universe was created for his exclusive enjoyment. We have superimposed the notion of evolution and progress over nature. Our mind (and there are no individual minds – only 'mind', which is the accumulation of the totality of man's knowledge and experience) has created the notion of the psyche and evolution. Only technology progresses, while we as a race are moving closer to complete and total destruction of the world and ourselves. Everything in man's consciousness is pushing the whole world, which nature has so laboriously created, towards destruction. There has been no qualitative change in man's thinking; we feel about our neighbours just as the frightened caveman felt towards his. The only thing that has changed is our ability to destroy our neighbour and his property.

Violence is an integral part of the evolutionary process. That violence is essential for the survival of the living organism. You can't condemn the hydrogen bomb, for it is an extension of the policeman there and your desire to be protected. Where do you draw the line? You can't. We have no way of reversing the whole thing.

Love and hate are exactly the same. They have together resulted in massacre, murder, assassination and wars. This is a matter of history, not my opinion. It is the same thing everywhere. All our political systems have come out of the religious thinking, whether of the East or the West. In the light of these facts, how can you have any faith in religion? What is the good of reviving the whole past, the useless past? It is because your living has no meaning to you that you dwell on the past. You are not even drifting. You have no direction at all; you are just floating. Obviously, there is no purpose to your life; otherwise you would not live in the past.

What has not helped you cannot help anybody. No matter what I am saying, you are the medium of expression. You have already captured what I am saying and making of it a new *ism*, ideology, and means to attain something. What I am trying to say is that you must discover something for *yourself*. But do not be misled into thinking that what you find will be of use to society, that it can be used to change the world. You are finished with society– that is all.

God is the ultimate pleasure, uninterrupted happiness. No such thing exists. Your wanting something that does not exist is the root of your problem. Transformation, *moksha*, liberation, and all that stuff are just variations on the same theme: permanent happiness. The body cannot take that. The pleasure of sex, for instance, is by nature temporary. The body can't take uninterrupted pleasure for long; it would be destroyed. Wanting to impose a fictitious, permanent state of happiness on the body is a serious neurological problem.

They sell you spiritual pethidine, spiritual morphine. You take that drug and go to sleep. Now the scientists have perfected pleasure drugs, which are much easier to take. It never strikes you that the enlightenment and God you are after is just the ultimate pleasure, a pleasure, which you have invented to be free from the painful state you are always in. Wanting two contradictory things at the same time causes your painful, neurotic state.

Meditation is itself evil. That is why all the evil thoughts swell up when you try to meditate. Otherwise you have no reference point, no way of knowing if the thoughts are good or evil. Meditation is a battle. The *gurus* promise you peace at the end of the battle, but you only experience more pain. I can assure you that not only is the goal of meditation and *moksha* put into you by your culture, but that ultimately you will get nothing but pain. You may experience some petty little mystical experiences, which are of no value to you or anyone.

What is the difference whether or not you find this freedom, this enlightenment or not. You will not be there to benefit from it. What possible good can this state do to you? This state takes away *everything* you have. That is why they call it *jivanmukti,* living in liberation. While living, the body has died. Somehow the body, having gone through death, is kept alive. It is neither happiness nor unhappiness. There is no such thing as happiness. This you do not, cannot want. What you want is everything; here you lose everything. You want everything, and that is not possible. The religions have promised you so much – roses, gardens – and you end up with only thorns.

That is all that is there. Go, look. I am only saying that you must find out for yourself if there is anything behind these meaningless abstractions being thrown at you. They talk of sacred hearts, universal minds, over-souls, you know, all the abstract, mystical terms used to seduce gullible people. Life has to be described in pure and simple physical and physiological terms. It must be demystified and de-psychologized.

Don't talk of 'higher centres' and *chakras*. It is not these but glands that control the human body. It is the glands that give the instructions for the functioning of this organism. In your case you have introduced an interloper—thought. In your natural state, thought ceases to control anything; it comes into temporary function when a challenge is put before it, immediately falling into the background when no longer needed.

That is why I am pointing these things out. Forget about the ideal society and the ideal human being. Just look at the way you are functioning. That is the important thing. What has prevented the organism from fully flowering into its own uniqueness is culture. It has placed that wrong thing – the ideal person – before man. The whole thing is born out of the divisive consciousness of mankind. It has brought us nothing but violence. That is why no two gurus or saviours ever agree. Each is intent upon preaching his own thing.

You come for the same reason you go to anyone for – answers. You believe that in knowing my story you will be able to duplicate what happened to me. You, having been brainwashed all your life, can only think in terms of imitation. You think that somehow you can repeat what happened to me, that is all. That is your motive for coming. It is not going to happen again through any activization or transference. This is not a new approach to that religious stuff. It is completely different. It has absolutely nothing to do with all that romantic, spiritual, religious stuff, nothing. If you translate what I am saying into religious terms, you are missing the point entirely. Religion, God, soul, beatitude, *moksha*, are all just words, ideas used to keep your psychological continuity intact. When these thoughts are not there, what is left is the simple, harmonious physical functioning of the organism. I am able to describe the way this organism is functioning because your question has created the challenge here. Your questions create the conditions necessary for this response to happen. So, it is describing itself, but that is not the way it is functioning. It functions in a state of not knowing. I never ask myself how I am functioning. I never question my actions, before, during or after they occur. Does a computer ask how it is functioning?

You can't fit me into that religious framework. Any attempt on your part to translate what I am saying into your religious framework is to miss the point. I am not one of your holy men who say, "I am hanging, so come hang with me." All that stuff is a form of madness.

Because just as the crazy woman there says she is not mad, you insist upon saying there is death, that you are going to die. Both are false. As far as being states of mind based upon reality, they are equally invalid.

Your intellectual understanding, in which you have a tremendous investment, has not done one damn thing for you so far. You persist in the cultivation of this intellectual understanding, knowing all the while that it has never helped you at all. *This is amazing.* When hoping and attempting to understand is not there, then life becomes meaningful. Life, your existence, has a tremendous living quality about it. All your notions about love, beatitudes, infinite bliss, and peace only block this natural energy of existence. How can I make you understand that what I am describing has absolutely nothing to do with all that religious stuff? You see hundreds of bodies carried off in the van after death, and yet you can't possibly imagine your own death. It is impossible, for you cannot experience your own death. It is really something. It is no good throwing all this junk at me. Whatever hits this is immediately burnt; that is the nature of the energy here.

The spiritual people are the most dishonest people. I am emphasizing that foundation upon which the whole of spirituality is built. I am emphasizing that *there is no spirit*. If there is no spirit, then the whole talk of spirituality is nonsense. You can't come into your own being until you are free from the whole thing surrounding the concept of 'self'. To be really on your own, the whole basis of spiritual life, which is erroneous, has to be destroyed. It does not mean that you become fanatical or violent, burning down temples, tearing down the idols, destroying the holy books, like a bunch of drunks. It is not that at all. It is a bonfire inside of you.

It is the ones who believe in God, who preach peace and talk of love, who have created the human jungle. Compared to man's jungle, nature's jungle is simple and sensible! In nature animals don't kill their own kind. That is part of the beauty of nature. In this regard man is worse than the other animals. The so-called 'civilized' man kills for ideals and beliefs, while the animals kill only for survival.

There is no such thing as truth. The only thing that is actually there is your 'logically' ascertained premise, which you call the 'truth'.

I renounce the only thing worth renouncing – the idea that there is renunciation at all. There is nothing to renounce. Your mistaken ideas regarding renunciation only create more fantasies about 'truth', 'God', etc.

Because man is worse than the animals, it made it necessary and possible for him to create the moral dilemma. When man first experienced the division in his consciousness – when he experienced his self-consciousness – he felt superior to other animals, which he is not, and therein sowed the seeds of his own destruction.

You can't experience anything except through thought. You can't experience your own body except through the help of thought. The sensory perceptions are there. Your thoughts give form and definition to the body, otherwise you have no way of experiencing it. The body does not exist except as a thought. There is one thought. Everything exists in relationship to that one thought. That thought is 'me'. Anything you experience based on thought is an illusion.

The word 'awareness' is misleading. Awareness is not a divided state; there are no two states – awareness and something else. They are not two things. It is not that you are aware of something. Awareness is simply the action of the brain. The idea that you can *use* awareness to bring about some happier state of affairs, some sort of transformation, or God knows what, is, for me, absurd. Awareness cannot be used to bring about a change in yourself or the world around you.

All this rubbish about the conscious and the unconscious, awareness, and the self, is all a product of modern psychology. The idea that you can use awareness to get somewhere psychologically is very damaging. After more than hundred years we seem unable to free ourselves from the psychological rubbish. Just what exactly do you mean by consciousness? You are conscious, aware, only through thought. The other animals use thought – the dog, for example, can recognize its owner – in a simple manner. They recognize without using language. Humans have added to the structure of thought, making it much more complex. Thought is not yours or mine; it is our common inheritance. There is no such thing as your mind and my mind. There is only *mind*– the totality of all that has been known, felt, and experienced by man, handed down from generation to generation. We are all thinking and functioning in that 'thought sphere', just as we all share the same atmosphere for breathing. The thoughts are there to function and communicate in this world sanely and intelligently.

The knowledge – that is all that is there. The 'me', 'psyche', 'mind', 'I', or whatever you want to call it is nothing else than the totality of the inherited knowledge passed on to us from generation to generation, mostly through education. You teach the child to distinguish between colours, to read, to imitate manners. It is relative to each culture. Americans learn American manners; Indians learn Indian manners, etc. Gestures of the body, hands or face constituted the first language. Later words were added on. We still use gestures to supplement our spoken words because we feel that words alone are inadequate to fully express what we want to convey.

All this is not to say that we can really know anything about thought. We can't. You become conscious of thought only when you make it an object of thought, otherwise you don't even know you are thinking. We use thought only to understand something out there, to remember something, or to achieve something. Otherwise, we don't even know if thought is there or not. Thought is not separate from the movement of thought. Thought is action, and without it you cannot act. There is no such thing as pure, spontaneous, thought-free action at all. To act is to think.

You have a self-starting, self-perpetuating mechanism, which I call the *self*. This does not mean that there is actually an entity there. I do not want or mean to give that connotation to the word. Where is this ego, or self, that you talk of? Your non-existent self has heard of spirituality and bliss from someone. To experience this thing called bliss you feel you must control your thoughts. It is impossible; you will burn yourself and die if you attempt it.

The demand for more and more experience constitutes your 'present', which is born out of the past. Look here is a microphone before you. You are looking at it. Is it possible for you to look at it without the word 'microphone'? The instrument you are using to look at and experience the microphone is the past, your past. If that is seen, there is no future at all. Any achievement you are interested in is in the future. The only way that the future can come into operation is in the present moment. Unfortunately, in the present moment what is in operation is the past. Your past is creating your future; in the past you were happy or unhappy, foolish or wise, in the future you will be the opposite.

When the past is not in operation there is no 'present' at all, for what you are calling the 'present' is the past repeating itself. In an actual state of 'here and now', there is no past in operation

and, therefore, no future. I do not know if you are following me...
the only way the past can survive and maintain its continuity is
through the constant demand to experience the same thing over
and over. That is why life has become a bore. Life has become
boring because we have made of it a repetitive thing. So, what we
mistakenly call the 'present' is really the repetitive past projecting
a fictitious future. Your goals, your search, your aspirations are
cast in that mould.

From your knowledge, out of the past, you ask questions,
and the very motive of your asking is only to gain more knowledge
from someone else so your knowledge structure can continue.
You are really not interested in this at all. Your knowledge coming
to an end means that *you* are coming to an end. Where, you ask,
is this knowledge, the past? Is it in your brain? Where is it? It is all
over your body. It is in every cell of your body.

All these questions spring from your search. It doesn't matter
what the object of that search is —God, a beautiful woman or
man, a new car. It is all the same search. And that hunger *will
never be satisfied*. That hunger must burn itself out completely
without knowing satisfaction. The thirst you have must burn itself
out without being quenched. It dawns on you that that is not the
way, and it is finished.

What I am emphasizing is that we are trying to solve our
basic human problems through a psychological framework, when
actually the problem is neurological. The body is involved. Take
desire. As long as there is a living body, there will be desire. It is
natural. Thought has interfered and trying to suppress, control,
and moralize about desire, to the detriment of mankind. We are
trying to solve the 'problem' of desire through thought. It is thinking
that has created the problem. You somehow continue to hope and
believe that the same instrument can solve your other problems as
well. You hope against hope that thought will pull you through, but
you will die in hope just as you have lived in hope.

Unless you are free from the desire of all desires, *moksha*, liberation, or self-realization, you will be miserable. The ultimate goal, which society has placed before us, is the one that has to go. Until you are free from that desire, you cannot be free from any of your miseries. By suppressing these desires, you are not going to be free. This realization is the essential thing, going as it does to the crux of the problem. It is society that has placed the desire for freedom, the desire for liberation, the desire for God, the desire for *moksha* –that is the desire you must be free from. Then all these other desires fall into their own natural rhythm. You suppress these desires only because you are afraid society will punish you if you act on them, or because you see them as 'obstacles' to your main desire – freedom.

If this kind of thing should happen to you, you will find yourself back in a primeval state without primitivity, and without any volition on you part. It just happens. Such a free man is not in conflict with society anymore. He is not antisocial, not at war with the world; he sees that it can't be any different. He doesn't want to change society at all; the demand for change has ceased. Any doing in any direction is violence. Any effort is violence. Anything you do with thought to create a peaceful state of mind is using force, and so, is violent. Such an approach is absurd. You are trying to enforce peace through violence. *Yoga*, meditation, prayers, *mantras* are all violent techniques. The living organism is very peaceful; you don't have to do a thing. The peacefully functioning body doesn't care one hoot for your ecstasies, beatitudes or blissful states.

Man has abandoned the natural intelligence of the body. That is why I say – it is my 'doom song' – that the day man experienced that consciousness that made him feel separate and superior to the other animals, at that moment he began sowing the seeds of his own destruction. This warped view of life is slowly pushing the entire thinking towards total annihilation. There is nothing you can do to halt it.

I am not an alarmist. I am not frightened; I am not interested in saving the world. Mankind is doomed anyway. All I am saying is that the peace you are seeking is already inside you, in the harmonious functioning of the body.

Anything you do to free yourself from anything for whatever reason is destroying the sensitivity, clarity and freedom that is already there.

There is no question of your seeing things as they are. You can't see things as they are. You never leave any experience or feelings you have alone. You have to capture and interpret that feeling within the framework of the known. You are happy or unhappy only as you have knowledge about and the experience of happiness and unhappiness. So, everything has to be brought within the framework of the known before you can experience it. The movement of the known is gathering momentum within you. Its only interest is to continue. There is no entity, no Self there to give itself continuity; it is just the movement of thought, the self-perpetuating separation. It is mechanical. Anything you try to do about it only adds momentum to it.

It is the desire to reach a particular goal, an all-important goal, that must go, not the countless petty little desires. The only reason you try to manipulate or control the petty desires is as part of your strategy to attain the highest goal, the desire of all desires. Eliminate that main goal and the others fall into a natural pattern and pose no problem for you or the world. You won't get anywhere by trying to endlessly control, manipulate or control these numerous desires. It is vicious in its nature.

The so-called 'highest goal' is like the horizon. The more you move towards it, the further it recedes. The goal, like the horizon, is not really there. It is a projection of your own fear and moves away from you as you pursue it. How can you keep up with it? There is nothing that you can do. Still, it is desire that keeps you moving; no matter in which direction you move, it is the same.

What you experience through your separative consciousness is an illusion. You can't say that falling bombs are an illusion. It is not an illusion, only your experience of it is an illusion. The reality of the world that you are experiencing now is an illusion. That is all I am trying to say.

There is no such thing as an absolute. It is thought, and thought alone, that has created the absolute. Absolute zero, absolute power, absolute perfection, these have been invented by the holy men and 'experts'. They kidded themselves and others.

Down the centuries the saints, saviours and prophets of mankind have kidded themselves and everybody else. Perfection and absolutes are false. You are trying to imitate and relate your behaviour according to these absolutes, and it is falsifying you. You are actually functioning in an entirely different way; you are brutal, you feel you must be peaceful. It is contradictory, that's all I'm pointing out.

The certainty that dawned upon me is something that cannot be transmitted. It does not mean that I am superior, a chosen one, one in whom all the virtues are rolled into one. Not at all. I am just an ordinary man and have nothing to do with it. This certainly blasts everything, including the claims of the so-called enlightened ones selling things in the marketplace.

What I am trying to put across is that there is no such thing as God. It is the mind that has created God out of fear. Fear is passed on from generation to generation. *What is there is fear, not God.* If you are lucky enough to be free from fear, then there is no God. There is no ultimate reality, no God-nothing. Fear itself is the problem, not 'God'. Wanting to be free from fear is itself fear.

You see, you love fear. The ending of fear is death, and you don't want *that* to happen. I am not talking of wiping out the phobias of the body. They are necessary for survival. The death of fear is the only death.

The man who practises virtues is a man of vice. Only such a man, a man of vice, would practise virtue. There is not a virtuous man in the world. All men will be virtuous *tomorrow*, until then they remain men of vice. Your virtue only exists in the fictitious future. Where is this virtue you are talking of? It is no good hoping to be virtuous in a future life either; there is no guarantee that there is any future life, much less that you will be free in it.

You are blind. You see nothing. When you actually do see and perceive for the first time that there is no self to realize, no psyche to purify, no soul to liberate, it will come as a tremendous shock to that instrument. You have invested everything in that – the soul, mind, psyche, whatever you wish to call it – and suddenly it is exploded as a myth. It is difficult for you to look at reality, at your actual situation. One look does the trick; you are finished.

I don't care. I am ready to go. I don't see anything other than the physical activity of the body. Spirituality is the invention of the mind and the *mind is a myth*.

Your traditions are choking you. But unfortunately, you don't do anything. You actually love being choked. You love the burden of the cultural garbage-sack; the dead refuse of the past. It has to drop away naturally. It just drops. You don't depend upon knowledge anymore, except as a useful tool to function sanely in this world.

Wanting has to go. Wanting to be free from something that is not there is what you call 'sorrow'. Wanting to be free from sorrow is sorrow. There is no other sorrow. You don't want to be free from sorrow. You just think about sorrow, without acting. Your thinking endlessly about being free from sorrow is only more material for sorrow. It (thinking) does not put an end to sorrow. Sorrow is there for you as long as you think. There is actually no sorrow there to be free from. Thinking about and struggling against 'sorrow' is sorrow. Since you can't stop thinking, and thinking is sorrow, you will always suffer. There is no way out, no escape…

Hope Is for Tomorrow, Not Today

Seeing today demands action; seeing tomorrow involves only hope.

Have you questioned this goal of yours, which makes *sadhana* necessary? Why take it for granted that there is such a thing as 'peace of mind'. Maybe it is a false thing. I am just asking the question to understand what particular goal you have.

When do you expect to have it? It is always tomorrow, next year, why? Why does tranquillity, or quietness of the mind, or whatever you choose to call it, only happen tomorrow, why not now? Perhaps this disturbance, this absence of tranquillity, is caused by the very *sadhana* itself.

That instrument called thought, which you are employing to achieve your so-called spiritual goals, is the result of the past. Thought is born in time, functions in time, and any results it seeks are bound to be in and of time also. And time is postponement, the tomorrow.

Take for example the fact of selfishness. It is condemned, while selflessness, a pure creation of thinking, is to be sought after. Its realization, however, lies always just ahead, tomorrow. You will be selfless tomorrow, or the next day, or, if there is one, in the next life. Why is it not possible for you to be totally free from selfishness now, today? And do you really want to be free from selfishness? You do not, and that is why you have invented what you call selflessness, in the meantime remaining selfish. So, you are not going to be selfless at all, ever, because the instrument that you use to achieve that state of selflessness or peace of mind is

(25)

materialistic in value. Whatever you do to be free from selfishness will only strengthen and fortify it. I am not saying that you should therefore be selfish, only that thinking about its abstract opposite, which you have called 'selflessness,' is useless.

You have also been told that through meditation you can bring selfishness to an end. Actually, you are not meditating at all, just thinking about selflessness, and doing nothing to be selfless. I have taken that as an example, but all other examples are variations of the same thing. All activity along these lines is exactly the same. You must accept the simple fact that you do not want to be free from selfishness.

You are using effort to be in an effortless state.

But why are you putting it off until tomorrow? You have to face the situation *now*. What do you want ultimately?

Suppose I say that this meaninglessness is all there is for you, all there can ever be for you. What will you do? The false and absurd goal you have before you is responsible for that dissatisfaction and meaninglessness in you.

Do you think life has any meaning? Obviously you don't. You have been told that there *is* meaning, that there *must* be a meaning to life. Your notion of the 'meaningful' keeps you from facing this issue, and makes you feel that life has no meaning. If that idea of the meaningful is dropped, then you will see meaning in whatever you are doing in daily life.

Whatever you want, even the so-called spiritual goal, is materialistic in value. What, if I may ask, is so spiritual about it? If you want to achieve a spiritual goal, the instrument you use will be the same that you use to achieve materialistic goals, namely *thought*. You don't actually do anything about it; you just think. So you are just thinking that there must be some purpose, some meaning to life. And because thought is matter, its object – the spiritual or meaningful life – is also matter.

Spirituality is materialism. In any event you don't *act*, you just think, which is to postpone. You *assume* that the goal is there. You have invented the goal to give yourself *hope*. But hope means tomorrow. Hope is necessary for tomorrow, not today.

You want more knowledge so you can develop better techniques for reaching your goal. You know that there is no guarantee that more experience, more knowledge, more systems and more methods will help you reach your goal. Yet you persist; it is all you know how to do. Seeing today demands action. Seeing tomorrow involves only hope.

You want to see meaning in your life. As long as you persist in searching for a purpose or meaning to life, so long whatever you are doing will seem purposeless and meaningless. The hope you have of finding meaning is what is causing the present state of meaninglessness. There may not be any meaning other than this.

The energy you are devoting to the search, to techniques, to your *sadhana*, or whatever you wish to call it, is taking away the energy you need to live. You are obsessed with finding meaning in life, and that is consuming a lot of energy. If that energy is released from the search for meaning, it can be used to see the futility of all search. Then your life becomes meaningful and the energy may be used for some useful purpose. Life, the so-called material life, has a meaning of its own. But you have been told that it is devoid of meaning and have superimposed a fictitious layer of 'spiritual'. How the hell can you use effort to be in an effortless state? You think that you can live an effortless life through volition, struggle and effort. Unfortunately, that is all you can do. Effort is all you know. The 'you' and everything it has achieved, has been as a result of effort. Effortlessness through effort is like peace through war. How can you have peace through war?

The 'peace of mind' you want is an extension of this war of effort and struggle. So is meditation warfare. You sit for meditation while there is a battle raging within you. The result is violent, evil thoughts welling up inside you. Next, you try to control or direct these brutal thoughts, making more effort and violence for yourself in the process.

Your attempt to control or suppress your thoughts only tires you out, making you sort of battle-weary. That is the effortlessness and peace of mind you are experiencing. It is not peace. If you want techniques for thought control, you have come to the wrong man.

Understanding your goal is the main thing. To achieve that goal implies struggle, battle, effort, will, that is all. There is no guarantee that you will reach your goal.

Here there is no need to sit in special postures and control your breath. Even while my eyes are open, in fact no matter what I am doing, I am in a state of *samadhi*. The knowledge you have about *samadhi* is what is keeping you away from it. *Samadhi* comes after the ending of all you have ever known, at death. The body has to become like a corpse before that knowledge, which is locked into every cell in the body, ceases.

Your highly praised inventiveness springs from your thinking, which is essentially a protective mechanism. The mind has invented both religion and dynamite to protect what it regards as its best interests. There is no good or bad in this sense. All these bad, brutal, terrible people, who should have been eliminated long ago, are thriving and successful. Don't think that by pretending to be spiritually superior you are avoiding any complicity. You are the world; you are *that*. This is all I am pointing out.

Why should life have any meaning? Why should there be any purpose to living? Living itself is all that is there. Your search for spiritual meaning has made a problem out of living. You have been fed all this rubbish about the ideal, perfect, peaceful, purposeful way of life, and devote your energies to thinking about that rather than living fully. In any case you are living, no matter what you are thinking about. Life has to go on.

You are living. As soon as you introduce the question 'how to live?' you have made a problem of life. 'How' to live has made life meaningless. The moment you ask 'how', you turn to someone for answers, becoming dependent. He then takes you for a ride.

There is nothing to be achieved, nothing to accomplish. Because you have created the goal – say, selflessness – you remain stuck in selfishness. If the goal of selflessness is not there, are you selfish? You have invented selflessness as an object to pursue, meanwhile continuing to be selfish. How can you ever end your selfishness as long as you pursue selflessness? A certain amount of practical selfishness is necessary for survival, of course, but with you it has become a tremendous, unsolvable problem.

You can't come into your own uniqueness unless the whole of human experience is thrown out of your system. It cannot be done through any volition or the help of anything. And then you are on you own.

It requires courage. But it is not courage in the usual sense. It is not the courage you associate with struggle or overcoming. The valour I am talking about is the courage that is naturally there when all this authority and fear is thrown out of the system. Courage is not an instrument or quality you can use to get somewhere. The stopping of doing is courage. The ending of tradition in you is courage.

When once you are freed from the pairs of opposites – right and wrong, good and bad – you will never be wrong. But until then the problem will be there.

It is like accidentally touching a live wire. You are much too frightened to touch it through your own volition. By sheer accident this thing touches you, burning everything... It burns out this search, the hunger. The hunger stops temptations in the future, *tomorrow*, but what about now?

There is no love in the world. Everybody wants the same thing. Whosoever is the most ruthless gets it – as long as he can get away with it. Getting what you want in this world is a relatively easy thing, if you are ruthless enough.

I had everything a man could want, every kind of desirable experience, and it all failed me. Therefore, I can never recommend my 'path' to anyone, having eventually faced the falseness of that path myself and rejected it. I would never even hint that there was any validity in all those experiences and practices.

The saints, saviours, priests, *gurus*, *bhagavans*, seers, prophets and philosophers were *all* wrong, as far as I am concerned. As long as you harbour any hope or faith in these authorities, living or dead, so long this certainty cannot be transmitted to you. This certainty somehow dawns on you when you see *for yourself* that all of them are wrong.

When you see all this for yourself for the first time, you explode. That explosion hits life at a point that has never been touched before. It is absolutely unique. So, whatever I may be saying cannot be true for you. The moment you see it for yourself you make what I am saying obsolete and false. And it is not because the hunger is satiated. The hunger can never be satiated, especially by the traditional food that is offered. With the burning away of that hunger, the duality ceases. That is all.

You are incapable of listening to anyone. You are the medium of my expression. I respond to your questions; I have nothing of my own. The expression of what is here occurs because of you, not me. That medium (you) is corrupted, so whatever I may say to you is corrupt. The medium is only interested in maintaining its own continuity. So, anything that happens there is already dead.

My interest is not to knock off what others have said (that is too easy), but to knock off what I am saying. More precisely, I am trying to stop what you are making out of what I am saying. This is why my talking sounds contradictory to others. I am forced by the nature of your listening to always negate the first statement with another statement. Then the second statement is negated by a third, and so on. My aim is not some comfy didactical thesis, but the total negation of everything that can be expressed.

You sense a freshness, a living quality in what is being said here. That is so, but this cannot be *used* for anything. It cannot be repeated. It is worthless. All you can do with it is to try to organize it; create organizations, open schools, publish holy books, celebrate birthdays, sanctify holy temples, and the like, thus destroying any life it may have had in it. Such things can help no individual. They only help those who would live by the gullibility of others.

My explanation is that there was an outburst of energy, which is utterly different from the energy that is born out of thinking. All spiritual, mystical experiences are born out of thought. They are thought-induced states, nothing more. The energy here that is burning all thought as it arises tends to accumulate. Eventually it has to escape. The physical limitations of the body act as obstacles to the escape of this unique energy.

When it escapes it goes up, never down, and never returns. When this extraordinary energy – which is atomic – escapes, it causes tremendous pain. It is not the pain you are familiar with. It has nothing to do with it. If it did, the body would be shattered. It is not matter converting into energy; it is atomic. The process goes on and on, while the pain comes and goes. It is like the tremendous relief when a tooth is extracted. That is the kind of relief that is there, not the spiritual. The translation of this as bliss or beatitude is very misleading. Through thought anyone can create those experiences; but it is not actually bliss. The real thing is not something that can be experienced. Anything you can experience is old. That means everything you experience or understand is tradition.

In other words, I am trying to free you not from the past, the conditioning, but rather, from what *I* am saying. I am not suggesting any way out because there is no way. I have stumbled into this and freed myself from the path of others. I can't make the same mistake they did. I will never suggest that anyone use me as a model or follow in my footsteps, my path can never be your path. If you attempt to make this your path, you will get caught in a rut. No matter how refreshing, revolutionary or fantastic, it is still in a rut, a copy, a second-hand thing. I myself do not know how I stumbled into this, so how do you expect me to give it to another? My mission, if there is any, should be, from now on, to debunk every statement I have made. If you take seriously and try to use or apply what I have said, you will be in danger.

You take for granted that they are what they say they are. I say it cannot be transmitted to another because there is nothing there to transmit. Neither is there anything to renounce. What is it that these teachers suggest you should renounce? Even your scriptures, the *Kathopanishad*, say that you must renounce the very search itself. The renunciation of renunciation happens not through practice, discussion, money, or intellect. These are the least of things. A tough translation of the original Sanskrit is, 'Whomsoever it chooses, to him it is revealed,' if this is so, then where is the room for practices, *sadhana*, and volition? It comes randomly, not because you deserve it.

If you are lucky enough to have this dawn on you, you will die. It is the continuity of thought that dies. The body has no death; it only changes form. The ending of thought is the beginning of physical death. What you experience is the emptiness of the void. But there is no death for the body at all. I am sure this is of little consolation to you, though. Just wanting to be free of egoism is insufficient; you must go through a clinical death to be free from thought and egoism. The body will actually get stiff, the heartbeat slows, and you will become corpse-like.

Whatever answers are given regarding death, you are not satisfied and must invent theories about reincarnation. What is it that will reincarnate? Even while you are alive, what is there? Is there anything beyond the totality of the knowledge that exists inside you now? So, is there death at all, and if there is, can it be experienced?

The ideas you have about that natural state are totally unrelated to what it actually is. You are trying to capture and give expression to what you hope is that state. It is an absurd exercise. What is there is only the movement to capture, nothing else. All the rest is speculation.

A Jolt Of Lightning

The very instrument that we are using to free ourselves
from the thing called 'mind' is the mind.
This understanding hits you like a jolt of lightning.

If there is anything like super consciousness or higher consciousness that people speak of, you are as much an expression of that as any of the claimants to that cosmic power. Every dog, every cat, every pig, every cow, the garden slug there, you, everybody, even Chengiz Khan and Hitler, and me are an expression of the same thing. Why should nature or some cosmic power, if there is one in the world, need the help of somebody as an instrument to express itself and help others?

I don't want to go into that in great detail. But what I have been emphasizing is that whatever happened to me happened despite everything I did. Whatever I did or did not do, and whatever events people believed that led me into this [natural state] are totally irrelevant. It is very difficult for me to fix a point now and tell myself that this is me, and look back and try to find out the cause of whatever has happened to me, because this is not in the field of cause-and-effect relationship. That is why I am emphasizing and overemphasizing all the time that it is acausal. That is very difficult for people to understand.

It is something like, to use my favourite phrase, 'Lighting hitting you – a jolt of lighting hitting you', and you don't know what you are left with. You have no way of finding out for yourself and by yourself what has happened to you. Has anything happened to me at all? But one thing I can say with certainty is that the very thing that I searched all my life was shattered to pieces. The goals that I had set for myself – self-realization, God-realization, transformation, radical or otherwise, or even enlightenment – were all false, and there was nothing there to be realized, and nothing to be found there. The very demand to be free from anything, even from the physical needs of the body, just disappeared, and I was left with nothing. Therefore, whatever comes out of me now depends upon what you draw out of me.

I have actually and factually nothing to communicate, because there is no communication possible at any level. The only instrument we have is the intellect. We know, in a way, that this instrument has not helped us to understand anything. So, when once it dawns on you that this is not the instrument, and that there is no other instrument with which to understand anything, you are left with this puzzling situation that there is nothing to understand. In a way, it would be highly presumptuous on my part to sit on a platform and try to tell people that I have something to say, that I have come into something extraordinary, which nobody has come into.

But what I am left with *is* something extraordinary – extraordinary not in the sense that it has been possible for me through any effort or volition of mine, but in the sense that everything that every man thought, felt, and experienced before is thrown out of my system. So, you can say that it is, indeed, a courageous thing that has happened to me. But I cannot tell people that through courage you can put yourself into that kind of situation.

It is very difficult to tell people how it all happened to me. They are only interested in finding out how it happened to me; because their only interest is to find out the cause, find out what led me into this. But when I tell them that it is acausal, it is very difficult for them to understand and accept it. Their interest is to find out a cause and make it happen to them.

You see when I was listening to JK it suddenly dawned on me, "Why the hell have I been listening to this man? From this description I feel that I am in the same state as that man." I said to myself that I was in the same state as that man, assuming for the moment that he was in the same state that he was describing and in the same state that the great spiritual teachers were in. "What the hell have I been doing all my life? Why the hell am I sitting here listening to him?" I then walked out with just a single thought whirling in me, as it were, like in a whirlpool. "How do you know that you are in the same state?" I understand that the question implies that I was familiar with the descriptions of various states. I had tried to simulate them in me and experience them, and that is all there is to it. So, this question went on and on. But suddenly this question also disappeared. I said to myself that there is no reason for me to feel grateful to anybody, to express my thanks to anybody.

Whatever has happened to me has happened despite listening to this teacher or that teacher, or doing this, that, or the other. But if I say all this, it is something which is not very interesting to people. The want to *know*, and I tell them that I myself do not know. I cannot look at myself and tell myself that I am an enlightened man, that I am a free man, that tremendous changes have taken place in me. So, I use this phrase that we very often hear on the commercials. It is not something like "before and after wash"; no washing has helped me to reach anywhere. It is just a happening. I still have to use the word 'happening', because there is no other way that I can communicate this and give a feel of this to anybody else.

Anything we simulate and try to experience is only from where we stand today. And where we stand today is the product of experiences of all kinds. So, anything we experience, although we call it rebirthing or trying to experience what it was like when we were a newborn baby or an infant, is naturally coloured by where we stand today. Anything we experience has no relevance, no meaning to what I am trying to say.

There are many people who talk of rebirthing. It has become fashionable for people to indulge in that kind of fantasy. You know in Japan they have some techniques in which by manipulating certain nerves at the base of your head they will make you go through the experience of your own birth. I have always maintained that the experiencing structure is totally absent at the time of our birth. And, I always questioned the psychologists, especially Freud, when he made the statement that birth is a traumatic experience, I don't think that it is a traumatic experience at all, because there is no experiencing structure there at all. Actually, it is very difficult to say as to when the experiencing structure in babies comes into operation. I am one of those who believe that the influence of environment is very limited on us. (I maintain that I am not an authority on such things). But the experiencing structure is genetic in its origin and in its expression. Everything is genetically controlled. If we really want to change individuals, the only way we can do it is not by changing the environment, not through changing the cultural input, but by trying to understand what really is the part that genes play in us. Maybe through some kind of genetic engineering we can create perfect human beings.

I am at the same time conscious of the fact that it is a very dangerous thing that we are indulging in. When once we perfect these engineering techniques, we will hand them over to the state. Thereafter it will be a lot easier for the state to manipulate individuals and turn them into mere robots. (I am not against robots, as we are actually robots, whether we like it or not). The state will make people do things, which they are unwilling to do. Usually it takes a lot of time and a lot of brainwashing to teach something to people – to make people believe in God, to make people believe in a particular political ideology. Conversely, to free them from some kind of belief we have to brainwash them all over again. It is a very elaborate and long process. But it is a lot easier and faster for us to use these techniques of genetic engineering to change individuals than it is possible otherwise.

I don't want to say anything about J. Krishnamurti. I don't have any idea of what happened to him. I don't know what he meant when he said he had no memory of what happened to him. Actually your memory becomes extraordinary after this happening. But the problem that we have to face today is different. We have been using our memory a lot. I always maintain (you may question this, and the experts in the field of brain psychology may question it; but one of these days they will have to accept what I am trying to say) that the brain plays a very minor role in the functioning of the body. It is not a creator at all. It is just a reactor. What this memory is we really don't know yet. One of these days the experts who are dealing with this problem of memory will have to come out with answers to questions like what these neurons are.

I maintain that memory is not located in any particular area of the body. Every cell in our body is involved. And my feeling is that we have come to a point in the history of mankind where we have to confront the problem of people who have lost their memories. We have put our memory and our brain to such use for which they are not intended. This is one of the reasons why we find that Alzheimer's Disease, or whatever you want to call it, is on the increase. The other day I heard that one in two of those in the eighty-year-old bracket are affected by it. You know recently there was also a report of the same disease in England. Six hundred thousand people are affected by this problem there.

Misusing memory. Using memory for purpose for which it is not intended. After all, what are you? You are a memory. We have to use memory in order to survive in the world created by our society, culture, or whatever you want to call it. There is no other way. I know that it is an extension of the same survival mechanism. No doubt it is.

When you burn your finger, you withdraw it at once. Automatically. There you don't have to use your memory. That is the way this human body is functioning. But to survive in this world that we have created, our world of culture, society, or whatever you want to call it, the constant use of memory is essential. The whole of our education is built on the foundation of how to develop our memory. I am afraid that I am going off on a tangent here!

I usually hop, jump, and skip. Let me try to stick to this point, which I am trying to make. Unfortunately, humanity has placed before itself the model of a perfect man. The idea of the perfect man is born out of the value system that we have created. That value system is born out of the behaviour patterns of the great teachers of mankind.

Jesus, Buddha, and all the great teachers are examples. Every human body, however, is unique. Nature is not interested in creating a perfect being. Its interest is to create only a perfect species.

Every one of us is unique, that implies that our code of enlightenment, if there is such a thing, would also be unique so that each of us reaches that state individually and uniquely. That is what I am trying to emphasize. It is just not possible for us to produce enlightened people on an assembly line. You know, if we look at history, even a country like India which prides itself as a land of spirituality has produced only a very few enlightened people. You can count them on your fingers. But unfortunately, in the market place, we have many claimants who say that are enlightened, and they are in turn out to enlighten everybody. There is a market for that kind of thing. The demand and supply principal is responsible for that. But actually an enlightened man or a free man, if there is one, is not interested in freeing and enlightening anybody. This is because he has no way of knowing that he is a free man, that he is an enlightened man. It is not something that can be shared with somebody, because it is not in the area of experience at all.

There is no such thing as a new experience. Suppose you go to a new place. What goes on in your mind, if I may use the word, is that you are always trying to fit whatever you are seeing into the framework of the past. The moment you say that something is new, it is the old that is telling you that it is new. So, it is very difficult for us to experience anything new because, if there is something really new, it is not in particular frames that the old is destroyed, but the totality of the past is destroyed in one great big blow.

You may not agree with me, but brush this aside as absurd and nonsense. But there is no such thing as a new experience. There is nothing new at all. It is the old that tells us that it is new, and through this gimmick thought is making what it calls new part of the old, and is thus maintaining its continuity. So, whatever you cannot experience does not exist. It may sound very dogmatic assertion on my part, but when you try to experience something that you have not experienced before, the whole movement of the experiencing structure comes to an end.

When I went to see Ramana Maharshi, I asked him, "Whatever it is you have, can you give it to me?" And he said, "I can give it, but can you take it?" Unfortunately, that is the traditional answer that is dished out by all the spiritual teachers. What is reported in the so-called story of my life is a garbled version of what I actually felt at that time. Anyway, anything I say today is irrelevant, because I don't know what I felt at that particular moment, and there is no way I can relive that experience from here, I said to myself. "What is it that he has? If there is anybody in this world who can receive it, it is I". I said this to myself and walked out. That, in a way, decided another phase of my life.

The old traditional approach to the whole question of enlightenment was thrown out of my system, although I continued to read books on religion, studied philosophy, psychology, and science. I tried to find out answers from those people who have not been contaminated by the traditional teachings. I got interested in Western philosophy and science, and tried to find out the answer to my basic question.

My basic question was one question: "Where is this mind that we are so concerned about, that we are trying to understand, study, and change? Why do we talk of a total change in the makeup of the mind? I don't see any such thing as mind there at all, let alone a transformation or mutation of the mind." This question always intrigued me and I questioned everybody about the mind. I tried to get answers from every area of human thought, but nothing helped me to find out the answers to those questions. At that time I didn't have the certainty that I have today. The certainty I have today that there is no mind is something which I cannot transmit to anybody, however hard I may try, because the very thing which we are using to communicate is in jeopardy, and you are not ready to accept that possibility.

The Buddhists also talk about no mind.They made a tremendous structure out of that philosophical thought. They talked of the void. They talked of emptiness. You know the whole Buddhist philosophy is built on the foundation of that 'no mind'. Yet they have created tremendous techniques of freeing themselves from the mind. All the Zen techniques of meditation try to free you from the mind. The very instrument that we are using to free ourselves from the thing called 'mind' is the mind. Mind is nothing other than what you are doing to free yourself from the mind. But when, once it dawns on you, by some strange chance or miracle, that the instrument that you are using to understand everything is not the instrument, and that there is no other instrument, it hits you like a jolt of lighting.

2.

LOVE

Love implies division, separation...

- ➢ Love Is Only A Trump Card
- ➢ Sex Is Painful To The Body
- ➢ The Build-up Of Sex And Love

Love Is Only A Trump Card

*When everything fails, you use the last card, the trump in
the pack of cards, and call it Love.*

Man is the same everywhere, yet there seems to be a
difference among them. The difference is artificially created by the
Western nations. They had the advantage of the technical know-
how, which was born out of the industrial revolution. When the
revolution went to America, with the help of that technical know-
how they exploited the resources of God's plenty there. You know
there was a time when anybody could go to the United States
without a passport. But in 1911 they introduced the necessity to
have a passport to enter the United States. In 1923 they introduced
the immigration laws. Once you are there in a particular place and
establish yourself and your rights, it is finished. (I am giving this as
an example, but this applies to every country.) If anybody lands
and colonizes any place on any planet, they will establish their
rights there and prevent all other nations from landing there. The
Americans established these same rights. It was God's plenty that
helped the nations to develop and hold on to what they have. But
they continue to exploit the resources of the rest of the world as
well as their own resources. Even today they are doing that. They
don't want to give up.

Basically, human nature is exactly the same whether in India
or in Russia or in America or in Africa. Human problems are
exactly the same. All the problems are artificially created by the
various structures created by human thinking. As I said, there is
some sort of (I can't make a definitive statement) neurological
problem in the human body. Human thinking is born out of this

neurological defect in the human species. Anything that is born out of human thinking is destructive. Thought is destructive. Thought is a protective mechanism. It draws frontiers around itself, and it wants to protect itself. It is for the same reason that we also draw lines on this planet and extend them as far as we can. Do you think these frontiers are going to disappear? They are not. Those who have entrenched themselves, those who have had the monopoly of all the world's resources so far and for so long – if they are threatened to be dislodged, what they would do is anybody's guess. All the destructive weapons that we have today are here only to protect that monopoly.

But I am sure that the day has come for people to realize that all the weapons that we have built so far are redundant and that they cannot be used any more. We have arrived at a point where you cannot destroy your adversary without destroying yourself. So it is that kind of terror, and not the love and brotherhood that has been preached for centuries, that will help us to live together. But this has to percolate to the level of human consciousness. (I don't want to use the word 'consciousness' or 'human consciousness' because there is no such thing as consciousness at all. I use that word only for purpose of communication.) Until this percolates to the level of human consciousness, in the sense that man sees that he cannot destroy his neighbour without destroying himself. I don't think it will help. I am sure that we have come to that point. Whenever and wherever you have an edge over your adversary or your neighbour, you will still continue to exercise what you have been holding on to for centuries. So, how are you going to solve the problem? All utopias have failed.

The whole mischief originated in the religious thinking of man. Now there is no use in blaming the religious thinking of man, because all the political ideologies, even your legal structures, are the warty outgrowth of the religious thinking of man. It is not so easy to flush out the whole series of experiences which have been accumulated through centuries, and which are based upon the religious thinking of man. There is a tendency to replace one belief with another belief, one illusion with another illusion. That is all we can do.

Because thought is violent, anything that is born out of thought is destructive. You may cover it up with all wonderful and romantic phrases: "Love thy neighbour as thyself". Don't forget that in the name of "Love thy neighbour as thyself" millions and millions of people have died, more than in all the recent wars put together. But we now have come to a point where we can realize that violence is not the answer, that it is not the way to solve human problems. So, terror seems to be the only way. I am not talking of terrorists blowing up churches, temples, and all that kind of thing, but the terror that if you try to destroy your neighbour you will possibly destroy yourself. That realization has to come down to the level of the common man.

This is the way the human organism is functioning too. Every cell is interested in its own survival. It knows in some way that its survival depends upon the survival of the cell that is next to it. It is for this reason that there is a sort of cooperation between the cells. That is how the whole organism can survive. It is not interested in utopias. It is not interested in your wonderful religious ideas. It is not interested in peace, bliss, beatitude, or anything. Its only interest is to survive. That is all it is interested in. The survival of a cell depends upon the survival of the cell next to it. And your survival and my survival depend upon the survival of our neighbour.

Love implies division, separation. As long as there is division, as long as there is separation within you, so long do you maintain that separation around you. When everything fails, you use the last card, the trump in the pack of cards, and call it Love. But it is not going to help us, and it has not helped us at all. Even religion has failed to free man from violence and from ten other different things that it is trying to free us from. You see it is not a question of trying to find new concepts, new ideas, new thoughts, and new beliefs.

As I said before, what kind of human being do you want on this globe? The human being modelled after the perfect being has totally failed. The model has not touched anything there. Your value system is the one that is responsible for the human malady, the human tragedy, forcing everybody to fit into that model. So, what do we do? You cannot do anything by destroying the value system, because you replace one value system with another. Even those who rebelled against religion, like those in the Communist countries, have themselves created another kind of value system. So, revolution does not mean the end of anything. It is only a revolution of our value system. So, that needs another revolution, and so on and so on. There is no way out.

The basic question that we all have to ask for ourselves is, what kind of a human being you want? The only answer to this human problem, if there is any answer, is not to be found through new ideas, new concepts, or new ideologies, but through bringing about a change in the chemistry of the human body. But there is a danger even there. When once we perfect genetic engineering and change the human being, there will be a tendency to hand this technology over to the state. It will then be a lot easier for them to push all the people into war and see that they kill each other without a second thought. You don't have to brainwash them. You don't have to teach them love or patriotism. Brainwashing takes a century, as brainwashing to believe in God took centuries. The Communists took decades to brainwash their people not to believe in God. But with genetic engineering, there is no need for that kind of brainwashing process. It is a lot easier to change human beings by giving just one injection.

Do you really think that there is freedom in the United States? What does that mean to a starving man – freedom of speech, freedom of worship, and freedom of the press? He does not know how to read the newspapers and is not interested in them. At least in the Communist systems they fed, clothed, and sheltered people, though that is now being denied to them in those nations. There is more unemployment than ever before in the Western countries. I don't think this is the model for the whole of mankind.

The whole system depends upon the exploitation of the resources of the world for the benefit of the Western nations. These laws that you are talking about are always backed by force. You know that the decision handed down by a judge is always backed by force. Ultimately, it is the force that counts. We all agree to submit ourselves to the decision of the judge. If you don't want to submit to them, the only recourse you have is to use violence. So all the gangsters get together and create a legal structure that is favourable to them. That they enforce on others through the help of violence, through the help of force.

What right do you have to create this blockade, for example, today around Iraq? What is the international law, which these people are talking about? I want to know. What happened when America attacked and occupied Granada, a small nation? Nobody ever objected to it; nobody ever created a blockade there. I am not impressed by the international law and its legal structure. As long as it is advantageous to you, you talk of law. When the law fails you use force.

There may be different schools of thought in the legal field as well, but that is only a theological discussion. You know what all the theologians indulge in – God is this, God is that, the Ontological, the Teleological and the Cosmological arguments for the existence of God. All these different schools of law are no different from the discussions of the theologians.

The institution of marriage is not going to disappear. As long as we demand relationships, it will continue in some form or other. Basically, it is a question of possessiveness. There was a time when I believed that economic independence for women would solve many of the problems in India. But when I visited America I was shockingly surprised that even those women who are economically independent wanted to possess their drunkard husbands. The husband was beating her everyday, and twice on Sundays. I know many cases. I am not generalizing, but possessiveness is the most important element. The basis of relationships is: "What do I get out of the relationship?" That is the basis of all human relationships. As long as I can get what I want, the relationship lasts.

The marriage institution will somehow continue because it is not just the relationship between the two, but children and property are involved. So it is not going to disappear overnight at all. And we use property and children as a pretext to give continuity to the institution of marriage. The problem is so complex and so complicated. It is not so easy for anybody to come up with answers to the age-old institution of marriage.

A lot of couples come to see me with their problems. Unmarried, unwed couples, if you listen to their stories, you cannot imagine their miseries. And yet they cannot part company. Unmarried couples are more miserable than married couples. The answer is not so easy. As long as we want to establish a relationship, so long this institution will remain. Maybe it will be modified, changed to suit the changing condition.

A leader of the feminist movement came to see me. She asked me, "What do you think of the feminist movement?" I said, "I am on your side; by all means fight for your rights. But remember that as long as you depend on a man for your sexual needs, so long you are not free. The other way round is also true: if you can satisfy your sexual needs with the help of a vibrator – that is a different matter. But if you want a man to satisfy you sexual needs, you are not free.

It is these institutions, which are responsible for the misery of mankind. There is no way you can change or modify these institutions. It is a lot easier for people in India now to go for a divorce than it was in earlier times. There was no question of me divorcing my wife or my wife divorcing me at that time. Now it is a lot easier. The changing conditions are responsible for a change in our ideas. But that does not mean that the problem has an easy and simple solution.

If people are ready to accept the misery, it is well and good. But it is a miserable situation. They are not happy with that. Total anarchy is a state of being rather than a state of doing. There is no action in total anarchy. It is a state of being. So why are we frightened of anarchy? The anarchy that you are talking about is the destruction of the institutions, which we have built with tremendous care, and of our belief that those institutions should continue forever. So, it is that we are fighting for – to preserve them in their pristine purity.

Why worry about the prospect of old age and the future of children when there is no family? It is society that has to take care of that problem. Why are you all paying taxes to the government if they don't do what they are supposed to do? It is the responsibility of each individual that he should do what he has promised to do. The problem is that once you put these individuals in the seat of power, then there is less chance of their sharing their power with others. And you provide them with tremendous weapons of destruction. A man like me who expresses this view will become the enemy of the state. They will not hesitate to destroy me. I don't care if I am destroyed. If they say, "Don't talk", I will stop talking. I don't believe in freedom of speech at all. If they say, "Don't talk", "what you are saying is a threat to mankind and to its institutions", "Good bye". I don't want to talk. I am not interested in changing the world. But they have promised to do certain things. You have elected them to the office; you have put them there in the seat of power and have unfortunately provided them with the most destructive of weapons. They will not hesitate to use them against you and me.

But these days there is no way you can use your nuclear weapons. I often say that if Bhutan invades India, India has no way of protecting itself. Bhutan is not going to invade India, unless it has the backing of some powerful nations. So, we are puppets of these people. We are spending so much money on defence. Defence against what? We talk of freedom of speech. If they say, "Don't talk", I am not interested in talking. I am not interested in saving individuals. And I am not interested in saving mankind.

I do not see any reason why anybody should starve on this planet. What are you doing to solve these problems? You may very well throw that same question at me. But I have not set myself up in the business of running this world. *They* have set themselves up in the business of ruling this or that country. What justification do you have for the fact that forty per cent of the people are allowed to starve in India today? It is not spiritual; it is not human either. It is inhuman to let your fellow beings starve. Religion has invented that wonderful thing called charity. Not only that; you don't stop there, but you give the Nobel Prize to somebody because of the charitable work that particular individual is doing. That is the most vicious and vulgar thing that the religious man has come up with today.

Everyone has a right to be fed. Nature has provided us with a bounty. But we are individually responsible for the inequities of this world. Don't ask me, "What are you doing about that?" I am not here running a crusade against these people. You have set yourself up to solve these problems. If you don't solve them, something is wrong not with the leaders but with the people who have put them there in the seat of power. If they don't do what they are expected to do, change those rogues. I have no business to tell someone how to run these governments; I am not running these governments at all. What business do I have to tell them that this is the way you should run the government? It is the responsibility of everybody to contribute his mite, his share. But the world remains exactly the way it has been forever. Nobody wants any change.

First thing, the state has to feed, clothe, and shelter everybody.

AIDS is another mistake we have made. One of the experiments went wrong. It is easy for us to blame the homosexuals, but the source of it is somewhere else.

Sex Is Painful To The Body

The moment there is a pleasurable sensation, the demand to extend it longer and longer is there. That is why there is this tremendous frustration there.

Sexuality, if it is left to itself, as it is in the case of other species, other forms of life, is merely a biological need, because the living organism has this object to survive and produce one like itself. Anything you superimpose on that is totally unrelated to the living organism. But we have turned that, what you call sexual activity, which is biological in its nature, into a pleasure movement.

There must be two, you know. I love somebody and somebody else loves me. Wherever there is division, there can't be love. We are trying to bridge this gap, which is horrible for us, which has no meaning, which is demanding something from us, with this fancy idea that there must be love between these two individuals.

Between whatever – I love my country, I love my dog, I love my wife, and what else, what is the difference – whether I love my wife, I love my country, or I love my dog? This may sound very cynical to you. The fact of the matter is that there is no difference. You love *your* country, I love *my* country, and there is war.

There is no love. Love is another of these thoughts. The body does not love itself. There is no separateness here.

Obviously, our relationships are not so loving. So, we want to, somehow, make them into loving affairs, loving relationships. What an amount of energy we are putting into making our relationship into a loving thing! It is a battle; it is a war. It is like preparing yourself all the time for war, hoping that there will be peace, eternal peace, or this or that. You are tired of this battle, and you even settle for that horrible, non-loving relationship. And you hope and dream one day it will be nothing but love. "Love thy neighbour as thyself"- in the name of that how many millions of people have been killed? More than all the recent wars put together. How can you love thy neighbour as thyself? It is just not possible. Otherwise, why are so many people, women, children, and helpless people killed?

When once love fails to establish the perfect ideal relationship between two individuals what we are left with is hate. If not hate, it is antipathy, apathy, or what other words…? My vocabulary is very poor.

Sexuality, if it is left to itself, as it is in the case of other species, other forms of life, is merely a biological need, because the living organism has this object to survive and produce one like itself. Anything you superimpose on that is totally unrelated to the living organism. But we have turned that, what you call sexual activity, which is biological in its nature, into a pleasure movement. I am not saying anything against the pleasure movement. It has become possible for us to have sex at any time we want through the help of thought.

Then it is a bore again. We have to write books – the *Joy of Loving*, the *Kama Sutra*, and all kinds of books – and make it interesting. It is not possible for animals to have sex at any time they want. Animals use it only for reproduction. Not that they 'use' it, but it is for the purposes of reproducing their own species. It is not a pleasure movement in their case. I am not saying anything against the pleasure movement. I am not interested in saying that you should condemn that or become promiscuous or use sex as a means of spiritual attainment. No.

It is a very simple functioning of the living organism. The religious man has turned that into something big, and concentrated on the control of sex. After that the psychologists have turned that into something extraordinary. All commercialism is related to sex. How do you think it will fall into its proper place?

I am not against that. Please don't get me wrong. I am just pointing out the use to which we are putting that simple biological function. I am not condemning it. It is there, you see. Your talk of that as an expression of love has no meaning to me.

Then there is no relation between love and sex. Most of the world thinks that love without sex is like a cold shake-hand. We would love to put it that way because it is very comforting. If sex is used only for the biological purpose, as I said, it is not really a devastating situation. If you leave it as it is, it wouldn't be so horrible, the way you would like to put it. It would fall into its proper place. That is why we have invented all these other things – God, truth, and reality – which are nothing but ultimate pleasures.

Whether you are here, in Russia, or anywhere else, the one thing that anybody and everybody wants in this world is to have happiness without one moment of unhappiness, pleasure without pain. That is just not possible, because this living organism does not know what pleasure is, what happiness is. It doesn't even want it.

It doesn't want it, because all these pleasurable sensations disturb it. The moment there is a pleasurable sensation, the demand to extend it longer and longer is there. That is why there is this tremendous frustration there. You want to make it possible for everybody that he should always be happy and that he should have only pleasant or pleasurable sensations and not any painful ones. It may be possible through some drugs like "ecstasy", but for how long? In the long run it destroys the sensitivity of the body.

You are not in living touch with anything there. So thought is separating us from the natural way.

The Build-Up Of Sex And Love

It is just not possible to have any relationship on any basis except on the level of mutual gratification.

Human relationships have become a kind of commercial exchange – in the sense of, "If you give me something, I will give you something". That's a fact. We do not want to accept it because it destroys the myth that human relationships are something marvellous and extraordinary. We are not honest, decorous and decent enough to admit that all relationships are built on the foundation of, "What I get out of this relationship." It is nothing but mutual gratification. If that is absent, no relationship is possible. You keep the relationship going for social reasons, or for reasons of children, property, and security. All this is part and parcel of the relationship business. But when it fails and does not give us what we really want, we superimpose on it what we call "love". So it is just not possible to have any relationship on any basis except on the level of mutual gratification.

The whole culture has created, for its own reasons, this situation for us through its value system. The value system demands that relationship be based on love. But the most important element is security and then possessiveness. You want to possess the other individual. When your hold on the other becomes weaker for various reasons, your relationship wears out. You cannot maintain this "lovey-dovey" relationship all the time.

The relationship between a man and a woman is based on the images that the two create for themselves of each other. So, the actual relationship between the two individuals is a relationship between the two images. But your image keeps changing, and so does the other person's. To keep the image constant is just not possible. So, when everything else fails, we use this final, last card in the pack, "love", with all the marvellous and romantic ideations around it.

To me, love implies two [persons]. Wherever there is a division, whether it is within you or without you, there is conflict. That relationship cannot last long. As far as I am concerned, relationships are formed and then they are dissolved immediately. Both these things happen in the same frame, if I may use that word. That is really the problem. You may think that I am a very crude man, but if anybody talks to me about love, to me it is a 'four-letter word'. That is the only basic relationship between man and woman. But it is a social problem for us as to what kind of a relationship you should have. Even in the days of my youth it was not possible amongst the Brahmins to marry unless the couple belonged to the same sub-caste. It was worse than the racial stuff in other countries. They had a strange idea of maintaining family traditions. What is tradition after all? It is unwillingness to change with the changing time. We change a little when we are forced to by conditions. But the fact is that change is not in the interest of the mechanism of our thinking.

Unfortunately, we have blown this business of sex out of proportion. It is just a simple biological need of the living organism. The body is interested in only two things – to survive, and to reproduce one like itself. It is not interested in anything else. But sex has become a tremendous problem for us, because we turned the basic biological functioning of the body into a pleasure movement. You see, if there is no thought, there is no sex at all.

The second problem is that it is not just the sex act that is important [to us], but the build-up that is there, the romantic structure that we have built around the love play. If you look at a beautiful woman, for example, the moment you say that it is a woman; you have already created a problem "A beautiful woman"!

Then it is more pleasurable to hold her hands than just to look at her. It is more pleasurable to embrace her, even more pleasurable to kiss her, and so on. It is the build-up that is really the problem. The moment you say that she is a beautiful woman; culture comes into the picture.

Here [me] the build-up is totally absent because there is no way that these eyes can be focused on any particular object continuously. For all you know, when that beautiful woman opens her mouth, she might have the ugliest teeth that a woman could have. So, you see, that the eyes have moved from there to here and again from here to something else, as perhaps, to her movements. It is [the eyes are] constantly changing its focus and there is no way that you can maintain this build-up. What is there is only the physical attraction. You can never be free from that. All those people – these saints – are tortured with the idea of controlling that natural attraction. But that natural attraction is something that should not be condemned. You don't tell yourself that you are a godman, a realized man, an enlightened man or a saint, and that you should not think these thoughts. That [telling yourself] is really the problem. They are not honest enough to admit that. So whenever a saint comes to me, or one who practises celibacy, I am very ruthless with him. I ask him, "Do you really mean to say that you never have wet dreams?" I tell him, "To practise celibacy in the name of your spiritual pursuit is a crime against nature." If the man is impotent or if for some reason the woman happens to be barren, then it is a different story. Why the religious thinking of man has emphasized denial of sex, as a means to his spiritual attainment is something that I cannot understand. Maybe because that is the way you can control people. Sex is the most powerful drive.

Sex is a very natural thing. You see, if you don't have sex, the semen probably goes out through your urine or in some other way. After all, the sex glands have to function. If they don't function normally, you are an abnormal individual. But we are not ready to accept these facts, because it undermines the very foundation of human culture. We cannot accept the fact that we are just biological beings and nothing more. It is something like saying that in the field of economics you are not controlled by the laws of supply and demand. But actually, in the field of economics you are. Likewise, in the political field the laws of politics control us. But we are not ready to accept the basic, fundamental fact that we are just biological beings, and all that is happening within the body is a result of hormonal activity. It is pure and simple chemistry. If there is any problem there [in the body], it is too presumptuous on my part to tell you that problems in that area cannot be solved in any other way than by trying to change the chemistry of the whole body. I think our whole thinking has to be put on a different track. I don't know; I am just suggesting. I may be wrong. I am not competent enough.

It is all chemical. If, as they say, desires are hormones, then the whole ethical code and culture that we have created through centuries to control the behaviour of human beings is false. Desire cannot be false. Anything that is happening within the [human] organism cannot be false.

There is no sex at all without thought. Thought is memory. These experts make fun of me when I say that the most important of all glands is the thymus gland. When I discussed this subject with some physiologists and doctors they made fun on me. Naturally so, because according to them, the gland is inactive. If it is activated through any external means, it would be an abnormal situation. But, you know, the thymus is the most important gland, and feelings operate there without the element of thought.

You see, medical technology has ignored that for a very long time. They considered any unusual condition of the gland to be an abnormality and tried to treat it. It is true that when you reach the adolescent age, it becomes inactive, and then your feelings are controlled by your ideas. Than by natural biology.

Feeling, to me, is like this: if you trip, I don't actually trip along with you; but the whole of my being is involved in that 'tripping over'. That is the kind of feeling that I am talking about; all other feelings are emotions and thoughts. The distinction between feeling [not in the sense that I mentioned just now] and thought is not really something… It is very artificial. It is cultural.

"The heart is more important than the head" and all such nonsense are absolute poppycock. When once this kind of disturbance takes place in the hormonal balance of the human body through this catastrophe, through this calamity, through whatever you want to call it, not only is the thymus activated but all other glands such as the pineal and the pituitary are also activated. People ask me, "Why don't you submit yourself to medical testing to validate all these claims?" I tell them that I am not selling these claims.

What I have against medical technology is that you want to understand the functioning of these things with a motive. When once you have some idea of how these glands function, how the activation of these things will help mankind, you are not going to use it for the benefit of mankind.

If you don't accept what I am saying, it is just fine with me. If some top physician wants to reject what I say, that fellow will say that I am talking rubbish. But now volumes have been written in America on the subject of the thymus gland. I am not claiming any special knowledge of these things. What I am trying to say is that the feelings felt at the thymus are quite different from the feeling induced by thoughts.

Sex has to be put in its proper place as one of the natural functionings of the body. It is solely, mainly and wholly for the purpose of reproducing or procreating something like this [the body]. It has no other place in the functioning of the body.

There is no way you can go back now, because thought always interferes with sex. It has become a pleasure movement. I am not saying anything against it. I go to the extent of telling people that if it is possible for you to have sex with your mother without any problem, psychological or spiritual, than that will put an end to your sex. You see, the whole thing is built on your ideas. I am not advocating incest as a way of life. For this [the body] there is no such thing as incest at all. It is the guilt problem, the psychological problem, the religious problem, which says that it has to be this way and not that way. If it is possible for a human being to have sex without a second thought, without any regret, with his sister, daughter, or mother, then this [sex] is finished once and for all. It falls into its proper place. I am not suggesting it as a therapy. Please don't get me wrong.

What I am trying to say is that it is just not possible to have sex with your wife or with anybody without the build-up. Sex goes after that. Thereafter, what you are left with is the natural functioning of the sex glands. If they are not used, the semen will go out through urine. All these claims of the spiritual teachers that it will move from the *muladhara* to the *sahasrara* are rubbish. Don't believe all that nonsense. If the semen is not used, it goes out through your urine whether you are a saint or a godman or a sinner. You may or may not have wet dreams, but still it goes out. The body still goes on functioning.

There seems to be an abnormal functioning here [with me]. What you call estrogen in the case of, what is that, I am not familiar with all these terms...the female hormones. You see, as they say, for the first few days or weeks, the sex of an embryo is not differentiated, but somewhere along the line, one becomes male. Here [in me] the body goes back into that stage where it is neither male nor female. It is not the androgynous thing that they talk about. It is more psychological. So, we have to revise all our ideas about this whole business of sex. We give a tremendous importance to sex, and so the denial of it becomes such an obsession with people.

In India they even moved away from that denial and created what is called Tantric sex. It was the highest pleasure that human beings could have. Sex through Tantra was considered the highest. That was the reason why they created in Brazil, and probably in some other countries too, the coupling of the male and the female organs. We have in India all that nonsense in the temples, and then a temple for the bull, a symbol of virility. All these were admired and worshiped. This is the other extreme [to denial of sex]: indulgence in sex became a spiritual pursuit. They talked of achieving spiritual goals, enlightenment, or what have you, through sex, and called it Tantric sex. Whether it is ordinary sex or Tantric sex, or you go and have sex with a prostitute, it's all the same.

At the moment of intense sexual involvement, or orgasm, people have the feeling that they are not there anymore... That feeling is temporary, very temporary. Not even a flash of a second. Even there, the division cannot be absent. Even in extreme grief you get the feeling that you are not there. What happens if the body goes through unbearable pain? You become unconscious. It is then that the body has a chance of taking care of that pain. If it cannot, then you go.

The fact is that the person is very much there even at the moment when there is peak sex experience. The experience has already been captured by your memory. Otherwise you have no way of experiencing that as a peak moment. If that peak moment remained as a peak moment; that would be just the end of sex; that would be the end of everything.

The fact that you remember it as a peak moment and want to repeat it over and over again implies that it has already become part of your experiencing structure. You want it always and then want to extend it for longer and longer periods of time. This is one of the most idiotic things to do. I read somewhere that a long time ago they tortured a woman to have a continuous orgasm for half-an-hour or one hour, I don't know. But why put her through that torture? What for? What do you prove by that? It is also a fad for people here in the West. They want to make it last longer. It is just for a fraction of a second, whether it is in the female or in the male. I think that there is really no justification for extending the orgasm longer that its natural duration. It has become an obsession with some people, and if they don't have it, their sex act seems very futile.

It becomes an addiction. Like any other addiction. All these things I observed myself. I did not learn about them from anyone. I saw them happen in my own life. I told my wife about them. Every time my wife talked of love I asked her what all that nonsense was about. The only basis of our relationship was sex.

I denied myself sex for twenty-five years pursuing spiritual goals. Then I suddenly realized, "Look, this is ridiculous. Celibacy has nothing to do with it. I have wet dreams. Sex is burning inside me. Why the hell am I denying myself sex? Why the hell am I torturing myself?" I asked my teacher, "Are you sure you didn't have wet dreams any time?" He blushed. He did not have the courage to give me an answer.

I had them. That did not mean that I moved to the other extreme and practised promiscuity as my way of life. The most beautiful girls from Holland, America, and everywhere surrounded me. I didn't even have to ask for it. But then, I felt that this was not the way to understand the problem of sex. The relationship with my wife was the only relationship I had then. She understood my attitude toward sex, but she still had some [of her own] ideas of love. She always asked me, "You are surrounded by the most beautiful women here. You are a very handsome man by any definition. Why don't you have sex with them? Do you have a problem of guilt or loyalty?" I told her, "Actually, if there is an act of infidelity on my part, the whole thing will change". I warned her, "Don't talk of all this nonsense. As a conversation piece, it's fine". It is not that there was a moral or ethical problem. I wanted to find out about sex, and I realized that I was actually using her for my pleasure.

And yes, we always discussed it. There was no love involved. Yet she was the finest woman I could have been married to. She also realized that that was all. But the only problem that we had was concerning children. She wanted more children because of her genes. My wife was the twenty-first pregnancy of her mother. And so, wanting more children was a genetic problem. That was the real problem between us. We even went to see Marie Stopes in London. You may have heard of her. My wife was also against birth control and such other measures. She tried to sort these things out. She was telling me that by nursing a child for a longer time, pregnancy could be delayed. All kinds of strange ideas! She was not ready to go to a doctor and finish it with an abortion. But somewhere along the line she did have an abortion, as we did not want to have more children.

Apart from all this, I did have a one-night stand. It was not with a cheap call girl or a prostitute. It was with one of the richest women around. And that finished the whole thing. There was no more sex after that. You will be surprised at that.

It just happened to me. I happened to be in this woman's place. I don't want to go into all the sordid details. That was thirty-three years ago. It was finished! That was the end of sex for me. I felt that I was using that woman for my own pleasure. It was not an ethical problem. The fact that I used that woman hit me very hard. I said to myself, "She may be a willing victim, a willing partner in this whole game, but I cannot do this any more." That was the end of it, and it created a problem for my wife also, not in the sense that she revolted against me but in the sense that I denied sex to her too.

She felt guilty for pushing me to that extent. It is not that she actually did that. She did not push me into that situation. Anyway, the incident finished sex for me. But that did not finish the sex urge per se, because just as in women there is a natural rhythm in men. I could notice that there was a peak sometimes, and for months and months you didn't even know about it.

Just like there is period for women. It is impossible for a woman and a man to attain orgasm at the same time. We are programmed differently. It cannot be synchronized. If that could be synchronized, it would be a marvellous thing. But there is no way you can do that at all. So, until this [the natural state] happened to me, the powerful drive [sex] was still there. But it knew that the semen would go through the urine or some other way. That didn't bother me because I was determined to figure out and solve this problem [of sex] for myself and by myself. I did not go to a therapist. I never believed in any therapy. So it resolved on its own and by itself. Sex has a place in the organism. It is a very simple functioning of the body. Its interest is only to create. I discovered these things by myself.

I will give you another example. We were about to make love, and my two-year-old girl cried. We had to break up, and you can't imagine what violent feelings I had that time. I just wanted to strangle that child! Of course, I did not act on those feelings. I could have. That was the frame of my mind. I said to myself, "That is the blood of my own blood, to use an idiotic phrase, bone of my bone – my own child. How can I have such thoughts? There is something wrong here [in me]." I told myself, "You are not a spiritual man, you are not what you think you are and what people think you are." I was lecturing on the Theosophical platforms everywhere. I said to myself, "You are 'this', and 'this' is you. This is what you are - all this violence."

Sex is violence. But it is a necessary violence for this body. It's a pain. All creative things are painful. The birth of a child is a very natural thing. But to call it a traumatic experience and build up a tremendous structure of theories around it is something I am not concerned with. It cannot be a traumatic experience. That is why, after all this violence you go to sleep. You feel tired. That is how nature functions. All creations in nature are like that. I don't call it pain or violence. Volcanic eruptions, earthquakes, storms, and overflowing rivers are all part of nature. You cannot say that there is only chaos or that there is only order. Chaos and order happen almost at the same time. Birth and death are simultaneous processes.

I am not against promiscuity, nor am I against celibacy. But I want to emphasize one basic thing, that is, in the pursuit of your spiritual matters it doesn't really make any difference whether you practise celibacy or indulge in sex and call it Tantric sex. It is comforting to believe that you are having Tantric sex and not sex with a call girl or a prostitute. To say that there is more 'feeling' or more closeness when you have sex for spiritual reasons is absolute gibberish.

There are so many people who are doing this kind of thing in the name of enlightenment. That is detestable to me. They are not honest enough to admit that they are using that [the lure of enlightenment] for fulfilling their lust. That is why they are running these brothels. These kinds of gurus are pimps.

Someone asked me, "What do you have to say about Rajneesh after his death?" I said that the world has never seen such a pimp nor will it ever see one in the future. He combined Western therapies, the Tantric system, and everything that you could find in the books. He made a big business out of it. He took money from the boys; he took money from girls, and kept it for himself. He is dead and so we don't say anything. *Nil nisi bonum* (Of the dead speak not unless it be good).

What I want to say is that unfortunately, society, culture, or whatever you want to call it, has separated the sex activity and put it on a different level, instead of treating it as a simple functioning of the living organism. It is a basic thing in nature. Survival and reproduction are basic things in the living organisms. And the rest is an artificial build-up...

You can change the areas, you can change the ideas, and you can write books. It really doesn't matter. As far as I am concerned, I don't tell anybody what he or she should or should not do. My interest is to point out that this is the situation and say, "Take it or leave it".

Anything we touch we turn into a problem; and sex even more so, because this is the most powerful drive there. If you translate it [into pleasure] and push it into an area where it does not really belong, namely, the pleasure movement, we will then create problems. When once you create a problem, the demand to deal with that problem within that framework is bound to arise. So, that is where you come in [with sex therapy etc.]. I have nothing against sex therapists, but the problem [sex as pleasure] has to be solved by people. Otherwise they become neurotic. They don't know what to do with themselves. Not only that, but everything, God, truth, reality, liberation, moksha, is ultimate pleasure. We are not ready to accept that.

But sex is very concrete. It is tangible. That is why it has become a very powerful factor in our lives. That is why there is also a demand to put limitations on it by culture, first in the name of religion, and then in the name of the family, law, war, and a hundred other things. This [the demand to limit sex] is nothing but the outgrowth of the religious thinking of man. What's the difference?

You talk of the sacredness of life and condemn abortion. This is the same old idiotic Christian idea persisting, which turned every woman into a criminal. And then you go on and kill hundreds and thousands of people in the name of your flag, in the name of patriotism. That is the way things are. Not that it is in your interest to change it, but change is something, which this structure [i.e., thought] is not interested in. It only talks of change. But you know things are changing constantly.

This artificial build-up of sexual excitement is actually damaging the body, but there are a lot of people who think that, because tension is released and you feel more relaxed, it is good for health. You first create a tension. All this fantasy, all this romantic nonsense, is building up tension. When once the tension is built, it has to dissolve itself. That is why rest becomes essential and you go to sleep. You fall asleep because you are tired and exhausted. The aftereffects are bound to follow. That's fine, but it's wearing you out in the long run.

Men using children and women as the object of sexual violence is a sociological problem. I can't say much about that problem. But it's really unfortunate that man got away with everything for centuries while society ignored women. Half the population of this planet was neglected, humiliated and treated as doormats. Even the Bible tells you that the woman is made out of the rib of man. What preposterous nonsense! You see, women's intelligence is lost for this culture. Not only here, it's the same everywhere.

The other party is also responsible for that. You are praising the woman as a darling and she accepts that minor role. The woman is also to be blamed for it. I am not overly enthusiastic about all these feminist movements today. It is a revolt that really has no basis; it's more of a reaction.

Both parties are responsible for the situation. I say this very often. One of the leaders of the feminist movement visited me and asked, "What do you have to say of our movement?" I said, "I am on your side, but you have to realize one very fundamental thing. As long as, you depend on man for your sexual needs, so long you are not a free person. If you use a vibrator for your sexual satisfaction, that is a different matter."

"You are very crude," she said. I am not crude. What I am saying is a fact. As long as you depend up on something or somebody there is scope for exploitation. I am not against the feminist movement. They ought to have every right. Even today, in the same job a woman is paid less in the United States than a man. Why?

There was a time when I believed that if women were to rule this world, it would be a different story. We had a woman prime minister in India and a woman prime minister in Sri Lanka. There was a lady prime minister in England. I don't know whether that will happen in America and whether a woman will be the president of the United States. But I tell you they [women] are as ruthless as any others. In fact, more ruthless. So this dream of mine was shattered [Laughs] when I saw that woman there in Jerusalem, what was her name... Golda Meir...

So, it is not a question of a man running the show or a woman running the show, but it is the system that corrupts. There wouldn't be any inherent difference between man and woman in this tendency to dominate anywhere and at any time. Power games are part of culture.

Now they are talking of hormones. I really don't know. They say it is the hormones that are responsible for the violence. If that is so, what do we do? Assuming for a moment that the advantage that we [men] have had for centuries is not a culturally instigated thing, but a hormonal phenomenon, you have to deal with it in a different way and not put that person on the couch, analyze him, and say that his mother or great-grandmother was responsible for his aggression. That is too absurd and silly. So, we have to find some way. The basic question that we have to ask ourselves is: what kind of a human being do you want? But unfortunately we have placed before ourselves the model of a perfect being. The perfect being is a godman or a spiritual man or an avatar, or some such being. But forcing everyone to fit into that mould is the cause of our tragedy. It is just not possible for us all to be like that.

Once upon a time, the sceptre and the crown, the church, and the pontiffs, were all worshiped. Later the kings revolted against that, and then the royal family came to be admired and worshipped. Where are they now? Others have eliminated royalty and have created the office of the president. We are told that you should not insult the head of the state. Until yesterday, he was your neighbour, and now he becomes the president of your republic. Why do you have to worship a king or a president? The whole hierarchical structure, whether of the past or of the present, is exactly the same.

But there seems to be a need in a person to seek for something which he thinks is higher that himself. That something is what we would like to be. That is why we admire and worship someone. The whole hierarchical structure is built on that foundation. It is all right with the politicians, let alone the monarchy and the church. Even the top tennis player or a movie star is a hero. They are models for us. And the culture is responsible for this situation. It is not only the physiological differences, the hormonal differences, if there are any, (I don't know and wouldn't know), but the whole commercialism has that effect. You walk into any store or watch any commercial on the television; they [the ad men] are always telling you how you should dress, and how you should beautify yourself. The beauty of a woman depends upon the ideas of Helena Rubenstein or Elizabeth Arden, or someone else. Now half the stores here contain cosmetics for men. I am not condemning it, but pointing out that that is the way of our life. So the ad man is telling you what kind of clothes you should wear, and what colours should match what other colours. He is telling you this all the time. So, you are influenced by what he is telling you. And you want what he wants you to want. How are we going to deal with this problem? I don't know. It is not for me to answer. It is for those people who want to deal with these problems.

Who is normal? The normal person is a statistical concept. But how can this [me] be a model? This [whatever has happened to me] has no value in the sense that whatever I am cannot be fitted into any value system. It is of no use for the world. It has no value for me and it has no value for the world. You may very well ask me the question, "Why the hell are we talking about all this?" Because you had some questions to throw at me, and what I am doing is to put them in a proper perspective. I only say, "Look at it this way".

I am not interested in winning you over to my point of view, because I have no point of view. And there is no way you can win me over to your point of view. It is not that I am dogmatic or any such thing. It is impossible for you to win me over to your point of view. During a conversation like this, somebody throws words at me like, "Oh, you are very this or very that". It is also a point of view. So how do you think these two points of view can be reconciled, and for what purpose do you want to reconcile them? You feel good because you have won him to your point of view. You use your logic and your rationality because you are more intelligent than I am. All this is nothing but a power play.

You feel good, like the people who claim to render service to mankind. That is the "do-gooder's high". You help an old woman across the street and you feel it is good. But it is a self-centred activity. You are interested only in some brownie points, but you shamelessly tell others that you are doing a social turn. I am not cynical. I am just pointing out that it [this feeling] is a do-gooder's high. It is just like any other high. If I admit this, living becomes very simple. If you admit this, then it also shows what a detestable creature you are. You are doing it for yourself, and you tell others and yourself that you are doing it for the benefit of others. I am not cynical. You may say that I am a cynic, but cynicism is realism.

The cynic's feet are firmly fixed on the ground.

Politics, economics, you name the field... It is exactly the same. We found ourselves in a situation where only spirituality mattered. And now there are movie stars instead of Jesus. So many people have movie stars, tennis players, or wrestlers as their models, depending upon what their particular fancy is. I visited a friend of mine. He was condemning his daughters for having the pictures of movie stars in the bathrooms. But when we walked into his living room, he had my photo on his table. I asked him, "What's the difference between the two?"

One day many Rajneesh disciples visited me in Mumbai. My host happened to be one of the top movie directors. He was very close to Rajneesh. He spent years and years practising all the techniques taught by Rajneesh. But after he met me he walked out on him. And in his living room, there used to be a massive picture of Rajneesh. After his encounter with me he removed it and put it in the cupboard and then put my picture there. Look what he has done!

Just like divorce in America. You divorce one woman and then the new wife comes. You put the old wife's picture and your children's pictures all in the attic and replace them with the pictures of the new wife's parents, grandparents and children.

Just see the absurdity of it. That is all that they can do replace one illusion with another illusion, one belief with another belief. But if the belief comes to an end, that's the end of everything.

There is nothing that one can do to change this. Not a thing. If you are lucky enough [I don't know, 'lucky enough' may not be the appropriate phrase], to find yourself where there is no attempt on your part to get out of the trap, then it may be a different story. But the fact of the matter is that the more you try to get out of the trap, the more deeply you are entrenched in it. This is very difficult to understand.

That's the trap - wanting to get out of it. I tell all those who want to discuss with me the question of how to decondition yourself, how to live with an unconditioned mind, that the very thing that they are doing is conditioning them, conditioning them in a different way. You are just picking up a new lingo instead of using the usual one. You begin to use the new lingo and feel good. That's all. But this is conditioning you in exactly the same way; that's all it can do. The physical body [of mine] is conditioning in such a way that it acts as intelligence. Conditioning is intelligence here. There is no need for you to think.

The conditioning of the body is its intelligence. That is the native intelligence of the body. I am not talking about the instinct. The intelligence of the body is necessary for its survival. That intelligence is quite different from the intellect that we have developed. Our intellect is no match for that intelligence. If you don't think, the body can take care of itself in a situation where it finds itself in danger. Whenever the body is faced with danger, it relies upon itself and not your thinking or your intellect. If, on the other hand, you just think, then you are frightened. The fear makes it difficult for you to act. People ask me, "How come you take walks with the cobras?" I have never done it with a tiger or any other wild animal. But I don't think I would be frightened of them either. If there is no fear in you, then you can take walks with them. The fear emits certain odours, which the cobra senses. The cobra senses that you are a dangerous thing. Naturally, the cobra has to take the first step. Otherwise, it is one of the most beautiful creatures that nature has created. They are the most lovable creatures. You can take a walk with them and you can talk to them. It is like a one-way seminar.

Once a friend of mine, a movie star, visited me in an ashram that I was staying in. She asked me whether it was all an exaggeration that cobras visited me and that I took walks with them. I said, "You wait till the evening or night, and you will be surprised". Later, when we went for a walk at dusk, not just one cobra, but its wife, children, and grandchildren - about fifteen of them, appeared out of nowhere. The whole family. My guest ran away!

If you try to play with it [with the idea of taking walks with cobras], you are in trouble. It is your fear that is responsible for the situation you find yourself in. It is your fear that creates a problem for the cobra; then it has to take the first step. If the cobra kills you, you are only one person. Whereas we kill hundreds and thousands of cobras for no reason. If you destroy these cobras, then the field mice will have a field day, and you will find that they destroy the crops. There is a tremendous balance in nature. Our indiscretions are responsible for the imbalance in nature.

If I find a cobra trying to harm a child or somebody, I would tell him (I may not kill the cobra, you see) or tell the cobra to go away. You know, the cobra will go away. But you, on the other hand, have to kill. Why do you have to kill hundreds and thousands for no reason? The fear that they will harm us in the future is what is responsible for such acts. But we are creating an imbalance in nature; and then you will have to kill the field mice also. You feed the cats with vitamins or a special kind of a food, and if the cat tries to kill a field mouse, sometimes you want to save the mouse. What for? Even cats do not eat mice any more, because they are used to the food from the supermarkets. But the cats still play with mice and kill them for no reason. They leave them uneaten in the fields. It's amazing. I noticed it several times.

They are corrupted cats. By associating themselves with us, even cats and rats become like human beings. You also give identity to the cats and names to the dogs. Human culture has spoiled those animals. Unfortunately, we spoil the animals by making them our pets.

This is your property, not mine. I have nothing to do with what I have said. It is you who have brought this out from me.

What you do with it is your affair. You have the copyright over whatever has come out. I don't sit here and think about these things at all. At no time do I do that. It doesn't concern me at all. You come here and throw all these things at me. I am not actually giving you any answers. I am only trying to focus or spotlight the whole thing and say, "This is the way you look at these things; but look at them this [other] way. Then you will be able to find out the solutions for yourself without anyone's help". That is all. My interest is to point out to you that you can walk, and please throw away all those crutches. If you were really handicapped, I wouldn't advise you to do any such thing. But you are made to feel by other people that you are handicapped so that they could sell you those crutches. Throw them away and you can walk. That's all that I can say. "If I fall…", that is your fear. Put the crutches away, and you are not going to fall.

When we are made to believe that we are handicapped, we become dependent on the crutches. The modern gurus supply you with mechanized crutches. The whole thing is put in there by culture. And you are giving life to it through constantly thinking about these things. You have a tremendous investment in all these things. But these are all memories, ideas.

I don't really know what memory is. We were told that, "To recall a specific thing at a specific time" is memory. We repeated this definition as students of psychology. But it is much more that that. They say that memory is in the neurons. If it is all in the neurons, where is it located in them? The brain does not seem to be the centre of memory. Cells seem to have their own memory. So, where is that memory? Is it transmitted through genes? I really don't know. Some of these questions have no answers so far. Probably one of these days they will find out.

I believe that the problems of this planet can be solved through the help of the tremendous high-tech and technology at our disposal. But the benefits that we have accrued through these advancements have not yet percolated to the level of all the people living on this planet. Technology has benefited only a microscopic number of people. It seems that even without the help of high-tech and technology it is possible for us to feed twelve billion people. When nature has provided us with such bounty, why is it that three-fourths of the people are underfed? Why are they all starving? They are starving because we are responsible for their problems. That is the problem that is facing us all today.

Even in Iraq it's the same. The game that is going on there is only to dominate and control the resources of the world. That is the naked truth and the rest of it is absolute rubbish. Whether you kill an Iraqi or an American it really doesn't matter. The president of the United States says, "I am ready to sacrifice Americans". For what? When the coffins start arriving in America, they will sing a different song. But that is not the point. I am not on this side or that. The reality of the situation is that.

The other problem is: how do we change a human being, and for what purpose? If the purpose is to correct physical deformities, we are lucky that medical technology will help us. If a child has some kind of handicap, there is something that can be done to change it. So, people have to be thankful to medical technology. Nature is not concerned about the handicap one way or another. One more person added to the population.

So, if any changes are necessary in human beings, and if you want them to function differently by freeing them from all the things that the ethical, cultural, legal structure is failing to free them from and thereby create a different kind of people, then probably only genetic engineering could come to our aid. Codes of ethics, morals, and the legal structure are not going to help. They have not helped so far. They have not achieved anything. But through the help of genetic engineering we may be able to free the individuals from the thieving tendencies, from violence, greed, and jealousy. But the question is, for what? I don't know for what?

The engineers are helped by the state. They are the victims of the state. They are doing this not, as they claim, for humanitarian reasons or altruistic purposes, but for recognition, for a Nobel Prize, or for some prestigious awards. So, if they find a solution, then… They will hand it over to the state, and it will become easier for the leaders to send people like robots to the battlefields and to kill without question. That is inevitable.

So what is it that we are actually doing? As I see it and this is my doomsday song - there is nothing that you can do to reverse this whole trend. Individually probably, you can jump off the tiger. But no matter what you say to that man who is frightened of jumping off and is continuing the tiger ride, it is not going to help him. Actually, you don't even have to jump off; you can continue to ride. There is no problem there. You are not in conflict with the society because the world cannot be any different. If someone wants to be on the top, if it is part of his power game, then he talks of changing the world; he talks of creating heaven or paradise on earth. But I want to know when.

During the Second World War we were all made to believe that it was a war to end all wars. What nonsense they talked! Has it ended wars? Wars have been going on and on. We were made to believe that the First World War was waged to make the world safe for democracy. Oh boy! We are all made to believe all kinds of stuff. If you believe your leader, or if you believe what the newspaperman is telling you, you will believe anybody and anything.

Why are you concerned about the world and the other man? You have not realized anything. If there is really that realization there is an action. I don't like to use the phrase "freed from all that", but you are not in conflict any more. There is no way you can bring the conflict [to an end]. The conflict is there because of the neurotic situation that the culture has put in you.

How do you realize? The intellect at your disposal is the one that is responsible for the neurotic situation. This is the human situation. There is no way you can resolve your problems through that instrument. But we are not ready to accept that it can only create problems and cannot help us to solve them.

To me, it is a fact. "It is so," means there is no further movement there to do anything about it. That is the end of the whole thing. It cannot be so for you. If it is so; that is the end of your dialogue. You are on your own.

You will not talk about me. If you talk about me it is just another story you are telling, picked up somewhere else. So what will come out of it is anybody's guess. What you will say will not be the same. If you are lucky enough to throw the whole thing out of your system, the whole of what everyone thought, felt and experienced...

You cannot, and there is nothing that you can do about it. You don't even complete that sentence. The situation is such that you don't even tell yourself that there is nothing that you can do about it. When you say to yourself that you can do nothing... Still that demand to do something is bound to be there. That is the problem. You call it hopelessness and say, "Intellectually I understand". But that is the only way you can understand anything. That is what you are trying to do now. I can say that that [thought] is not the instrument, there is no other instrument, and there is nothing to understand. How this understanding dawned on me, I really don't know. If I knew that, it would be as worthless as any other thing. I really don't know. So, you have to be in a situation where you really don't know what to do about this whole situation. You have not exhausted the whole thing. You know, if you exhaust one, there is always another one [situation], another one, and yet another one.

To attempt to free yourself from that, to put yourself in a state that you really don't know, is part of the movement [of thought].

3.

SOCIETY

The fear of extinction brings us together...

- ➤ Lost In The Jungle
- ➤ We Have Created This Jungle Society
- ➤ It's Terror, Not Love, That Keeps Us Together

Lost In The Jungle

When you stand still then what is there takes over and probably enables you to live in the midst of all these brutalities.

The demand to be prepared for all future actions and all situations is the cause of our problems. Every situation is so different; and our attempt to be prepared for all those situations is the one that is responsible for our not being able to deal with situations as they arise.

It is useless to speculate about it, but for some reason we are made to believe, or we have accepted the belief that has been passed on to us from generation to generation, that we are here for some grander purpose, for a nobler purpose than the other species on this planet. I maintain that we are here for no grander purpose than that of the garden slug out there or the mosquito that is sucking your blood.

I don't know that whether there is any such thing as evolution. Those who talk about evolution have made us believe that there is such a thing. We are told that if we look at the animal species that we have on this planet, there is only one and a half percent of what existed before. It you take the plants into consideration, what we have on this planet is only half a percent of what existed before. What, therefore, makes you think that the human species is more important than the other species that have become extinct? What has made it possible for us to survive, go on, and maintain the human species on this planet longer than others, is thought. It is thought that has made it possible for us to live longer than the other species.

(80)

But that is our enemy. Thought is our enemy. In the long run, our belief, hope, or faith that thought will help us by freeing us from the problems that it has created is just wishful thinking.

Thought is a protective mechanism. It is interested in protecting something. We use thought for the purpose of maintaining the continuity of thought. Anything that has come out of thought is protective in its nature. It is not interested in protecting the life around us. It has isolated us from the rest of the species on this planet. It has given us the idea that we are something different, that the whole thing is created for our purpose, and that we have a right to take advantage of this superiority over others, to do whatever we want to do on this planet.

I maintain and very often say that thought in its birth, in its content, in its expression, and in its action is fascist. It is very aggressive. I use the word 'fascist' not really in the sense that the politicians use, but to mean that thought is very aggressive. Our very demand to understand nature's laws is to use them for the purpose of maintaining the continuity of thought. All the talk that thought is altruistic and that we are curious to know the laws of nature just for the sake of knowing them is bluff. The very motivation, the drive behind our demand to understand the laws of nature is to use them for the purpose of continuing the human species at the expense of every other form of life on this planet.

If we did not have this kind of thought, probably we would have become extinct and nature would have created a better form of human species on this planet. We would do anything that the animals would not do. The survival of one form of life at the expense of another form of life is a fact in nature. But we kill other species for an idea.

We also kill ourselves for an idea and we kill others too. But that kind of thing you don't see happening in other forms of life, other species on this planet. We kill for an idea. The whole foundation of our culture and civilization is built on the idea of killing and being killed, first in the name of God as symbolized by all the religious institutions, and in the name of political ideologies as symbolized by the state. The whole foundation of culture is built on the idea of killing and being killed.

We are moving progressively in the direction of destroying everything. We somehow have tremendous faith that the thought, which has helped us to create everything that you sec and are very proud of, will help us to change the course of events. This faith, I maintain, is misplaced. Somehow we have a faith that this instrument, thought, which has helped us to be what we are today, will somehow help us to create a better, happier life on this planet.

Everything you discover is adding to the momentum of destruction. Everything, because, the drive behind that discovery is to use it for purposes of maintaining the continuity, the status quo.

We are doomed, you see. As I said at the beginning, we are lost in the jungle; we have tried every possible means of escape. But still, somehow, there is a faint hope that maybe there is some way we can get out of this jungle. But we just have to stand still and let things happen.

You cannot stand still. You cannot stand still because of the fear that you will be lost forever. But we don't seem to have the feeling that there is not a damn thing that we can do to get out of this jungle.

When you stand still then what is there takes over and probably enables you to live in the midst of all these brutalities. That life has a charm of its own. It will not bring you in conflict with society at all. You don't even want to change anything. The demand to change is born out of your isolation. When once you think that you can bring about a change in yourself, the demand to change the world is also there. But this human body is not interested in learning or knowing anything. All that is necessary for the survival of this living organism is already there. There is a tremendous intelligence there, and all that we have gathered and acquired through our intellect is no match for that.

Yes, the intelligence of the body knows. One of the things that I always emphasize and try to put across to those who are interested is that the human brain is not interested in anything that we are interested in, what the culture has imposed on us, in any of its ideation and mentations. The brain is so dull; you will be surprised. It is not interested in any experience of any kind. What it is interested in is to help the body function intelligently and sanely.

But unfortunately, we have put that brain to a use for which nature has not intended it. The brain is not a creator. It is only a reactor; it reacts to stimuli. The mechanism that we have implanted in it as it were, through our education and culture, has made us believe that it is a creator. All the thoughts that we are thinking are not self-generated. They are not spontaneous. They always come from outside, and the brain is there only to translate this sensation – the translation that is necessary for the survival of this living organism. It is not interested in any of the spiritual experiences or anything that the 'mind' is interested in. In fact, I don't see any mind there at all. The mind is interested only in sensuality. It is born out of sensuality. It maintains its continuity in the field of sensuality. So all religious experiences of any kind are sensual in their nature. It is only the mind that is interested in spiritual experiences – bliss, compassion, truth, reality, and all those kinds of things. But the body, the living organism, is not interested in any of those things but only to respond to stimuli.

There is no creativity in the sense in which we use the word 'creativity' – language, the creativity of thought, the creativity of this, that, or the other. Life is creative in the sense that it does not use any model. Anything we call creative is an imitation, copy of something that is already there. It is second hand. You cannot say that something which nature has created is not up to the point. I don't even see any blue print there. Whatever blue print is there is already there in the cell. Everything that is there now was there in that single cell. Everything is genetically controlled.

The idea that there is something that we can do to bring about a change within us and change in the world has placed us in a situation where we are left with a hope that somehow this may happen. You live in that hope and die in that hope.

What kind of change are you interested in? Change is possible in the physical world. For example, if you are not interested in the shape of a stubbed nose, you can go to a plastic surgeon and change it into an aquiline nose. If you feel that it is fashionable to have that then there is a possibility of availing the help of a plastic surgeon. Or, through genetic engineering it will be possible for us to bring about a change in behaviour patterns. I do not claim to have a special insight into the nature of things or an understanding of the workings of nature more than anybody else, but this is what I have discovered for myself. I don't care whether you accept what I am saying or not. It stands or falls by itself. I don't care for even the biologists, the psychologists, or scientists in general. If they brush this aside and say this is all absolute rubbish, it is fine with me. One of these days they are going to discover these things anyway.

You see, the discovery is not within the framework of thinking. In other words, there is no such thing as discovery. Discovery is a wrong word.

You experience what you already know. Otherwise, there is no experience at all. There is no such thing as a new experience. The so-called epoch-making discoveries in the field of science are not really epoch-making discoveries. Take, for example, Newtonian physics. It works very well for some countries. But that very Newtonian physics proved to be a stumbling block for making a 'quantum jump', if I may use the word. Somehow, somebody like Einstein was lucky to take the lead and discover something different.

Actually, it is not different. Unless you link up these two things – what was there before, and what you think you have discovered – there is no point in talking about that at all. The scientist is interested in linking up these things and producing some results. Otherwise the discovery has no value at all. Newtonian physics is valid, functional, and true within its own framework. But this same Newtonian physics is not so true, not so valid, compared to what we have (or rather, Einstein has) since discovered, namely, the 'theory of Relativity'. Of course, Newtonian physics is still valid within the framework of the scientific thinking of man. After all, we admire all these people and regard them with prestigious honour – the Nobel Prize, this, that, and the other. Do you know the reason why? It is because of the technology that has become possible through discoveries of these people. Otherwise, there is no such thing as true discovery. There is no such thing as pure science at all. I may be making a lot of dogmatic statements, but my statements stand or fall by themselves.

I very often use the phrase 'stumbled into'. Somehow, somewhere along my journey of discovery, it occurred to me that this instrument which we have been using, what we call the intellect, is not really the instrument to understand anything. But I was very clear that the only instrument we have to understand anything is the intellect, and that there is no other instrument. So, the whole of our discovery is nothing but improving...sharpening that intellect. That is all that is there. So, this (the intellect) has not helped me to understand the living problems of my life, nor understand myself and the world around me. The understanding that this is not the instrument and that there is no other instrument somehow dawned on me.

There is no instrument to understand anything other than this instrument. That knocks off the whole foundation of intuition or any other way of understanding the reality surrounding us. There is nothing to understand. That is why I maintain that there is no such thing as reality at all, let alone the ultimate reality. You have no way of experiencing the reality of anything – the reality that we have so much taken for granted. We don't experience anything other than what we know.

It is a repetitive process experiencing the same thing over and over again. That is why we are born hoping that one day we will find something extraordinary, some new experience. The moment you say that it is something, which you have not experienced before, that it is a new experience, it means that it has already become part of the past experiencing mechanism.

Boredom is there only when you think that there is something more interesting, more purposeful, more meaningful that you could do than what you are doing. I am never bored – how I got out of it, I wish I knew. That is why I used the phrase 'stumbled into'. There is no way I can communicate this to anybody. Anybody who comes and listens to me and tries to understand what I am trying to put across is wasting his time, because there is no way you can listen to anything without interpretation. The interpreter is the reference point, which is you. You are the product of the totality of all the thoughts, experiences, and feelings of every form of life that existed before you. Thought is only interested in maintaining its continuity and status quo. It does not want any change. It says that it wants to change but the change that it is interested in is only to maintain its continuity, its status quo. Although things are changing constantly, it does not want to accept anything that will disturb its status quo. Also the reference point is strengthened and fortified by interpreting what I am saying to you.

You don't want to accept that any attempt on your part to get out of that trap in which you find yourself is strengthening the shackles. And there is no way out. Accepting means that you are sick and tired of doing anything. But saying that does not really mean anything.

Why do we look for a purpose or meaning in life? Why? Why should there be any meaning? The question. "How to live?" is totally unrelated to the functioning of this living organism. It is living all the time. It doesn't have to ask the question, "How to live?" "How to live?" is superimposed on the living organism.

Obviously you do not see any meaning. You do not see any purpose in life. Obviously you don't see. I don't mean only you. I mean people. To me to ask that question is so silly, so meaningless, and so absurd – "What is the meaning of life?" It is not life that we are really interested in but living. The problem of living has become a very tiring business – to live with somebody else, to live with our feelings, to live with our ideas. In other words, it is the value system that we have been thrown into. You see, the value system is false.

We are trying to fit ourselves into that value system which is totally false. It is falsifying you. But you are not ready to accept that it is falsifying you. You throw a lot of energy into this business of fitting yourself into that framework or value system.

You ask, how does one get to that point wherein one is willing to accept that this is false. 'How' implies that you want to know from somebody. That is adding momentum to that – to know, to know, and to know. That is why we always ask that question, 'how?'. 'How?' means you want to know. What is this 'you', as you experience yourself? The 'you' as you know yourself is a product of the momentum of that knowledge that is passed on to us. It has this question that you think is a very intelligent question. Through your demand for an answer to that question it wants to know how to add momentum to that knowledge.

It knows that by asking the question it can add momentum to itself. It is not 'you', because 'you' don't exist. There is no individual there at all. Culture, society, or whatever you want to call it, has created 'you' and 'me' for the sole purpose of maintaining its own continuity. But at the same time we are made to believe that you have to become an individual. These two things have created this neurotic situation for us. There is no such thing as an individual, and there is no such thing as freedom of action. I am not talking of a fatalistic philosophy or any such thing. It is this fact that is frustrating us. The demand to fit ourselves into that value system is using a tremendous amount of energy, and there is nothing we can do to deal with the living problems here. All the energy is being consumed by the demands of the culture or society, or whatever you want to call it, to fit you into the framework of that value system. In the process, we are not left with any energy to deal with the other problems. But these problems, that is, the living problems, are very simple.

To survive in this world is not a difficult problem, you see. But what is demanding is the value system. Our efforts to fit ourselves into that value system are consuming a tremendous amount of energy.

I am not in conflict with this society. You seem to be in conflict with this society, but I am not, because it cannot be any different, since I have found out that there is no way I can bring about a change in it. You want to bring about a change in the world. You see, the problem is a problem of relationship. It is just not possible to establish any relationship with anything around you, including your near and dear ones, except on the level of what you can get out of the relationship. You see, the whole thing springs from this separation or isolation that human beings live in today. We are isolated from the rest of creation, the rest of life around us. We all live in individual frames. We try to establish a relationship at the level of "What do I get out of that relationship?" We use others to try and fill this void that is created as a result of our isolation.

We always want to fill this emptiness, this void, with all kinds of relationships with people around us. That is really the problem. We have to use everything, an idea, a person, anything we can get hold of, to establish relationships with others. Without relationships we are lost, and we don't see any meaning; we don't see any purpose. This is because your only interest is to create a purposeful and meaningful relationship with the individuals and the world around you. Therefore, you want to understand the reality of the world.

But there is nothing to understand. There is no such thing as reality at all. I have to accept the reality of the world as it is imposed on me by the society. Say, I call you a 'woman', I call this a 'bench', and I call this a 'tray'. Otherwise, we will not be able to function in this world sanely and intelligently. This kind of knowledge can be used only for the purposes of functioning in this world sanely and intelligently. Anything you do to understand the reality of the world is not going to be useful, helpful, or meaningful.

We Have Created This Jungle Society

Man has polluted, destroyed and killed off everything, all on account of his wanting to be at the centre of the universe, of all creation.

Basically, I don't see any future for man. It is not that I am a doomsayer, but rather that anything that is born out of division in men will ultimately destroy him and his kind. So I don't dream or hope for a peaceful world.

Because the inevitability of war is in you. The military wars out there are the extension of what is going on all the time inside you. Why is there a war waging inside you? Because you search for peace. The instrument you are using in your attempt to be at peace with yourself is war.

There is already peace in man. You need not search. The living organism is functioning in an extraordinarily peaceful way. Man's search for truth is born out of this same search for peace. He only ends up disturbing and violating the peace that is already there in the body. So what we are left with is the war within man, and the war without. It's an extension of the same thing.

Our search in this world for peace, being based upon warfare, will lead only to war, towards man's damnation.

Many philosophies, including Marxism, say that war and struggle are inevitable. True, it is inevitable. The Marxists and others posit a thesis, which, through struggle, becomes an antithesis, until a synthesis is finally reached. But one man's synthesis is another man's thesis, giving rise to a newly formulated antithesis, and so on. These are philosophical inventions devised to give life some coherence and direction. I, on the other hand, maintain that life may have started arbitrarily; it may have been put together by accident. Man's efforts to give life direction can only meet with frustration, for *life has no direction at all*.

But this does not imply that the missiles are on their way, that doomsday is just around the corner. Man's instinct for survival is very deep-rooted. What I am saying is that all this sweet talk of peace, compassion, and love has not touched man at all. It's rubbish. What keeps people together is terror. The terror of mutual extinction has had a strong and ancient influence upon man. This is, of course, no guarantee. I don't know.

The day man felt this self-consciousness in him, which made him feel superior to every other species on the planet, is the day he set out on the road to complete and total self-destruction.

If man is destroyed, probably nothing is lost. Unfortunately, the instruments of destruction he has been able to stockpile over the ages are getting worse and worse, more and more dangerous. *He will take everything with him when he goes.*

Its genesis was in the religious idea that man is at the centre of the universe, and everything is created for the benefit of man. That is why man is no longer a part of nature. He has polluted, destroyed and killed off everything, all on account of his wanting to be at the centre of the universe, of all creation.

I question the very existence, the very idea of the self, the mind, the psyche. If you accept the concept of the self (and it is a concept), you are free to pursue and gain self-knowledge. But we never question the idea of the self, do we? You are interested in the self, not I. Whatever it is, it is the most important thing for man as long as he is alive.

You have never questioned the basic thing assumed here. That is: *I think*, therefore, I am. If you don't think it never occurs to you that you are alive or dead. Since we think all the time, the very birth of thought creates fear, and it is out of fear that all experience springs. Both the 'inner' and 'outer' worlds proceed from a point of thought. Everything you experience is born out of thought, so everything you experience, or *can* experience, is an illusion.

The self-absorption in thought creates self-centeredness in man; that is all that is there. All relationships based upon that will inevitably create misery for man. These are bogus relationships. As far as you are concerned, there is no such thing as a relationship. And yet the society demands not just relationships, but *permanent* relationships.

I don't think you can put a label on me. The existentialist talks of despair and absurdity. But they have never really come to grips with despair or absurdity. Despair is an abstraction for them. These are abstract concepts on which they have built a tremendous philosophical structure. That's all there is to it. What I refer to when I talk of self-centred activity is an autonomous automatic self-perpetuating mechanism, entirely different from what they are theorizing about.

There is no question of a Self there, so how can the question of immortality, the beyond, arise? It is mortality that creates immortality. It is the known that creates the unknown. It is time that has created the timeless. It is thought that has created the thoughtless.

Because thought in its very nature is short lived. So every time a thought is born, you are born. But you have added to that the constant demand to experience the same things over and over again, thus giving a false continuity to thought. To experience anything you need knowledge. Knowledge is the entire heritage of man's thoughts, feelings and experiences, handed on from generation to generation.

Just as we all breathe from a common fund of air, we appropriate and use thoughts from the surrounding thought sphere to function in this world. That's all there is to it. Man's insistence that thought must be continuous denies the nature of thought, which is short-lived. Thought has created for itself a separate destiny. It has been very successful in creating for itself a separate parallel existence. By positing the unknown, the beyond, the immortal, it has created for itself a way to continue on. There is no timeless, only time. When thought creates time, a space is created there; so thought is also space as well. Thought also creates matter; no thought, no matter. Thought is a manifestation or expression of life, and to make of it a separate thing, impute to it a life of its own, and then allow it to create a future for its own unobstructed continuity, is man's tragedy.

I don't think that this kind of life exists anywhere else, on any other planet. I am not saying that there may not be life in other worlds, only that it is not like our existence here.

Your ruminations about other forms of life and other worlds are just a wish for unlimited extension into the future and far-off places. Thought is trying to give itself continuity, and speculation about the future and undiscovered worlds is a convenient way to do it! Your thinking determines what you can become conscious of, period.

People talk of 'passive awareness', journeys of discovery, psychological transformations, open schools and launch foundations. These activities do not free you, but perpetuate the movement of thought and tradition. There is no freedom of action for man. I am not talking of some cataclysmic, deterministic philosophy of resignation.

You can try all kinds of things, but it won't help. You will only succeed in creating disturbances within the body, disturbing the harmony that is already there. By bringing about strange hallucinations and unnatural metabolic changes you only harm the body. That's all there is to it. There is nothing you can do to reverse this, to change direction. Thought-induced reality cannot be denied; it is *there*.

In order to concentrate or focus on one thing you must block out the others. By concentrating upon what you take to be 'nothing', you withdraw and separate yourself from the natural flow of life through and around you. You are part of a generalized magnetic field and what separates you from others is thought. You are concerned only with *your* happiness and unhappiness, the video set *you* are watching.

The table is not an object at all. The very fact that you recognize the table as a table is the issue. It does not matter, as the philosophers seem to think, that you and I have slightly different views of the chair and so interpret it differently. Neither does it matter whether the chair is there when I leave the room. The philosophers go on and on about this. It is absurd. You view and experience things from a different viewpoint than others, that's all. You think that you are having a subjective experience of an objective thing. There is nothing here, only your relative, experiential data, your 'truth'. There is no such thing as objective truth at all. There is nothing that exists 'outside' or independent of our minds.

Since I assume that *I* exist, my neighbour also exists. But I am questioning this. Do I have any way of experiencing the fact of my existence? I really have no way of knowing if I am alive or dead. I could go to a doctor who will examine me, take my temperature, my pulse, my blood pressure, and he will tell me everything is normal. In this sense you are a living, animate being in contradistinction to the inanimate objects around you. But you have actually no way of experiencing *for yourself* and *by yourself* the fact that you are a living being.

There are two things. There is the body which feels the pain and the knowledge telling you, 'this is blood,' 'this is pain,' 'this is the cessation of pain.' There is pain, but there is no one there who feels the pain. There is nobody who is talking now. I am not making a mystical statement when I say such a thing. Talking is a mechanical thing, like a tape recorder. Your questions are like playing on the tape recorder here. Your questions draw out certain responses automatically.

Love, deep abiding feelings, profound responses to the beauty of nature – all is typical romantic stuff. Pure poetry! Not that I have any bone to pick with romanticism or poetry. Not at all. It just doesn't mean anything. You actually have no way of looking at the sunset because you are not separate from the sunset, much less writing poetry about it.

The extraordinary experience you have when looking at a sunset you want to share. Using poetry, music, or painting as a medium, you attempt to share your experience with another person. That's all there is to it. The actual sunset is beyond your experience structure to capture. The observer is the observed. You cannot separate yourself from what you see. The moment you separate yourself from the sunset, the poet in you comes out. Out of that separation poets and painters have tried to express themselves, to share their experiences with others. That is culture. Culture induces its own responses. There is *nothing* more to it.

You see, it all depends on what we mean by culture. That part of culture that promises you peace, bliss, heaven, *moksha*, and selflessness is the problem. To separate the rest of culture – how you entertain yourself, how you eat, your work habits and language – from this counter-reality created by culture is a mistake. The so-called savages are functioning in exactly the same way we are functioning today. Basically, there is no difference. In either the primitive or modern cultures there is no peace.

Man is *already* at peace with himself. The idea that there is peace somewhere else, sometime in the future, is causing the problem. All these religious experiences like compassion, bliss, love are part of the craving for a non-existent peace, which is destructive to the natural peace already there in the body. I am questioning the whole spiritual experience. That's what I am trying to rip apart.

Man has always wanted to entertain himself with something or the other. The rituals have provided him with the necessary entertainment over the years, and now movies, videos, television, circuses, talks and the whole lot have replaced them. There are so many of them, you see. Each one is trying to sell his own particular brand of cigarettes, his own particular commodity. We want them. There is a market for these spiritual commodities. That is why someone is selling them. Nobody can sell me that kind of stuff because I am not interested in it. Others may be.

Whatever is happening at the moment is all that is there for me. To explain it is very misleading. I don't know how to explain it. Look, I read science-fiction books. Why? Because there is action there. I am not interested in the outcome at all, only the ongoing action. It is like a striptease. It is the stripping I find interesting, not the ending. Who cares about endings? Similarly, all your yesterdays, all your knowledge, and your very sense of self are dead things of the past. These memories have a great deal of emotional content for you, but not for me. I am only interested in what is actually happening now. Not tomorrow or yesterday.

To me there is no present either, much less the future. What is there is only the past, nothing else. So your phrase 'the here-and-now' means nothing to me. I don't know if I make myself clear. If I recognize you and we carry on a conversation, it is only the past that is in operation. I am looking at things. If I recognize and name those things, the past is in operation. It is projecting what it knows. The future, although indeterminate, is a modified continuity of the past. So what is this 'now' you are talking about? There is no such thing as this moment. This moment is not a thing that can be captured, experienced, or given expression to. The moment you capture what you think of 'this moment' you have already made it a part of the past.

All this implies that we can never touch the same place at the same time and place; it is like two tape recording machines in a room playing old tapes to each other. So you have no way of communicating anything to anybody. So there is no communication at all. And when this is understood very clearly there is no *need* for communication at all.

For this reason man is denied any real freedom of action. You may prefer one kind of music or food over another, but that only reflects your own background and culture.

Why do you assume that *everything* must have a beginning, an ultimate cause? Cause and effect may be just a casual thing. Events may just occur, just happen. The whole process of evolution may be just another happening, a causeless event. Why must you insist that everything must have a creator, and that the whole thing *must* have sprung from some ultimate cause?

That is *your* assumption. There may not be any such thing as the Big Bang. They use that term in contradistinction to the concept of creation in a steady state. So these are two theories trying to establish themselves as truth. Each competes with the other, trying to present itself as the more plausible of the two. I am not against the scientific method *per se*. What I am pointing out is the fact that there is no such thing as a 'pure' search of knowledge for its own sake. Knowledge is sought, scientifically or otherwise, because it gives power.

Love is an invention of the moment, used to replace power. Since you have failed in every other way, through every other channel, to acquire that all-powerful state of being, you have invented what you call love.

Love, compassion are all born out of the divisive consciousness in man: ultimately it will end up defeating the very cause its working and dying for. The people around Mother Teresa are capitalizing on her fame. All they are interested in now is money, you know, to carry on her work. Why should all these things be institutionalized? You see someone in pain, or hungry. You respond to him. That's all there is to it. So, why should that be institutionalized? You corrupt that feeling, that immediate response, which is not just a thought or petty emotion, when you attempt to institutionalize generosity and empathy. It is the immediate response to the situation that counts. I don't see institutionalization as compassion. That's the only thing you can do in a given situation, and that's the end of it. Animals are helpful to one another to a surprising degree. Human beings are naturally helpful to each other. When institutionalization dulls that natural sensitivity, I say it is not compassionate. All events in my life are independent of all other events; there is nothing there lining them up or institutionalizing them.

First of all, I have no views at all. You see, they wanted me to go on television in the United States. They have a program called, 'Point of View,' I told them 'I have no point of view.' I have no particular message for mankind, nor do I have any of the missionary zeal in me.

I am not a saviour of mankind, or any such thing. People come here. Why they come is not my concern. They come out of their own free will and volition because they have heard of me or out of sheer curiosity. It doesn't matter. One person may come here out of any one of a number of reasons. He finds me somehow different, a rare bird, and cannot figure me out or fit me into any framework he knows. He tells his friends, and soon they arrive at the door. I can't tell them to get lost.

I invite them in, knowing very well that there is nothing I can do for them. What can I do for *you*? 'Come in, sit down, make yourself comfortable,' is all I can say. Some people make tape recordings of our conversations together. It is their concern, not mine. It is their property first of all, not mine.

I have no interest in asking the questions you are interested in. I have no questions of any kind, except those that help me to function in daily living: 'What time is it? Where is the bus stop?' That is all. These are the simple questions that are necessary to function in an organized society. Otherwise, I never ask any questions.

This is a jungle we have created. You can't survive in this world. Even if you try to pluck a fruit from a tree, the tree belongs to someone or to society. So you have to become a part of society. That's why I always say that the world does *not* owe a living to me. If I wish to enjoy the benefits of organized society, I must contribute something to it. This society has created us all. Society is always interested in the *status quo*, in maintaining its own continuity.

Lust is born out of the thought of that individual who is part and parcel of society. The actual genetic information, probably residing in each cell of the body, is also passed on and constitutes the basis of consciousness. What society is interested in is that we all contribute to the continuity of society, that we all perpetuate the *status quo*. Society will of course permit some slight modifications, but no more.

So, what does a man like me contribute to the society? Nothing, so how can I expect anything from the society? Society does not owe a living to me at all. On the other hand, what I am saying is a threat to the society as it is presently organized. The way I am thinking, functioning, and operating is a threat to the present society. If I really become a threat, this society will liquidate me. I am not interested in becoming a martyr or anything. It doesn't interest me at all. So, if they say, 'Don't talk,' fine, I don't *have* to talk.

If they expect me to be a martyr so as to revitalize their faith in themselves, they will be sadly disappointed. It is their problem, not mine. If they find me a menace to society, what can they do? They may torture me, as they do in the communist countries, so what? Would I continue to speak against the State then? I really don't know what I would do. I do not indulge in hypothetical situations.

I have views on every damned thing from disease to divinity because I have acquired all this knowledge through studies, travel, experience and the like. But my views are of no more importance than those of the maid cleaning and cooking there. Why should any importance be given to my views and opinions?

You may say that I am a well-read man, that, as a result of my reading, my travels, my conversations with intellectuals, scientists, philosophers, I have a right to express my views on everything. But nothing I say or believe is important. Do you understand that? All I am trying to point out is that all this knowledge you are so proud of flaunting isn't worth a tinker's damn.

Knowledge has become important to you because it gives you power. As I said at the very beginning, knowledge is power. *I know, you don't know*. I *have* religious experience and you *don't have* it. So it's all one-upmanship, showing off.

Whatever happened to me happened not because of, but in spite of my past. And that's a miracle. I really don't know. I am not a man of humility or any such thing. Looking back on the situation, I really have no way of telling you what it was all about. All I know is that I am free from my past, and thank heaven for that! It is understanding. It is knowledge, which has dawned upon me. I cannot communicate it; much less recommend it to others.

Humility is an art that one practices. There is no such thing as humility. As long as you know, there is no humility there. The known and humility cannot coexist. In saying this I am not giving you a new definition of humility. I believe there is no such thing as humility at all. I'm just not in conflict with society, so to create the opposite of the brutality in the world – humility – does not occur to me. Society cannot be anything other than what it is. So, since there is no demand to bring about a change *in* me, there is no corresponding demand to change the society. I am not a reformer. I am not a revolutionary either. In fact, there is no such thing as revolution. All that is bogus. It is another commodity to be sold in the marketplace, to hoodwink gullible people. In other words, there is no difference between the world of Gandhi and the world of Ho Chi Minh, or between the values Christ propagated and those Lenin fought for.

I have no worldview, no structure of thought, which can help you. Nothing helps me. This certainty I have is something that cannot be transmitted to anyone else. And yet this certainty has no value at all.

I stumbled upon it. You see, my grounding was in Madras, in the same kind of environment that produced J. Krishnamurti. Religious people, all kinds of strange people, surrounded me. I realized early that they were all fakes whose lives and preaching were miles apart. So it wasn't worth anything, as far as I was concerned. I know all about these saviours, saints, and sages. They have all cheated themselves and fooled everybody. But you may be sure that I am not going to be fooled by anybody. I am in a position to say they are *all* wrong.

The 'change', if that is the word you want to use, that occurred to me is a purely physiological event, with no mystical or spiritual overtones at all. Anybody who gives a religious slant to any physical happening like this is kidding himself and is kidding the whole of mankind. The more clever and cunning you are, the more successful you will be in persuading people.

So you acquire power from people, and then project it upon others. You get tremendous power from your followers, and then project it back on them. So it gives you the illusion that it is affecting everyone around you. You then come out with some ridiculous statement that this has affected the whole of human consciousness. Actually, it has no psychological or social content at all.

It is not that I am antisocial. As I have said, I am not in conflict with society at all. I am not going to destroy all the temples or churches, or burn any books. No such thing. Man cannot be anything other than what he is. Whatever he is, he will create a society that mirrors him.

You must find your basic question. My basic question was: 'Is there anything behind the abstractions the holy men are throwing at me? Is there really anything like enlightenment or self-realization?' I didn't want it; I just had this question. So naturally I had to experiment. I tried so many things, this, that and the other. For a while. Then you find out one day that there is *nothing* to find out at all! You reject them completely and totally. This rejection is not a movement of thought at all, not a superficial denial. It is not done to attain or achieve something.

There is nothing to get. There is nothing to find or to find out. The understanding that there is nothing to understand is all there is. Even that is an inferential statement. In other words, there is nothing to understand.

First of all, you see, you don't have the hunger, the thirst to find out the answer to that. So you can't do a thing about it. Anything you do perpetuates that, keeps your hunger at bay. What seems to have happened to me is not that my hunger has been satisfied, either with breadcrumbs or the whole loaf of bread, but that the hunger found no satisfactory answer and burned itself out. All these thirst-quenchers haven't helped to quench my thirst. But somehow in my case the thirst burnt itself out. I am a burnt-out case but not in the sense in which you use that term. It's an entirely different kind of being, burnt-out. What is there now is something living. There is no *need* for communication. No communication is possible on that level. The demand to know, to be certain, is not there at all.

It's just like the tree out there. What do you want to do with the trees? They are not even self-conscious that they are useful to other forms of life, providing shade… Like the tree, I am never conscious that I can be of any service to anyone.

The movement of desire is so fast that it doesn't stop there. There is something – I wouldn't say it's more interesting or more attractive – but it changes that movement and demands your complete attention. Everything happening at that moment demands your complete and total attention. In that state there are no longer two things: lover and beloved, pursuer and pursued. What you call 'a beautiful woman' – which is an idea – gives way to something else. And there comes a time when you can't love her in the old way anymore. The thought that she's a woman isn't there. Then you see what a beautiful woman can give you. 'What can I get from this woman', is not there. Everything is constantly moving. There is no religious content to this at all.

Inspiration is a meaningless thing. So many things and people inspire us, but the actions born out of inspiration are meaningless. Lost, desperate people create a market for inspiration. So I am not interested in inspiring anybody. All inspired action will eventually destroy you and your kind. That's a fact!

What do you want to prevent? In you love and hate are born. I don't like to put it that way because love and hate are not opposite ends of the same spectrum; they are one and the same thing. They are much closer than kissing cousins. If you don't get what you expect out of so-called love, what is there is hate. You may not like me to use the world 'hate', but it is apathy and indifference to others. I believe love and hate are the same thing. I tell this to people wherever I go, all over the world.

In the early days Jiddu Krishnamurti didn't have a huge organization like he has today. It was a small simple organization publishing a few books, that was all. He did a little travelling and public talking, organized informally by some friends. That was it. But now it is a Limited concern, a growing industry like any other business. This kind of organization he has now, with worldwide real estate holdings, boards of trustees, vaults of insured tape recordings, millions of dollars, all runs counter to his basic teaching, which is that you can't organize the truth. He shouldn't be building an empire in the name of spiritualism.

I've never been a shopper. I've encountered a few of them for a few minutes in my travels, that's all. What I am was born out of my own struggle. I learned everything about myself *by* myself. Both the secular and the spiritual schools of thought irritate me. The *gurus* and God-men are therefore, of no interest to me at all. We have exported them to the United Sates and Europe. They have their own too... The Reverend Moon, Jim Jones...And now there is another Jones: Da Jones, 'the one who gives' in *Sanskrit*. Any holy scam is welcome there, whether from Indonesia, Japan, India, or Nepal. If they get popular enough in the west, make enough of a splash; we bring them back to India. It is similar to how Indian women bring back *saris* from the west to wear here. They pay three times the price there!

I am not in touch with what's going on in India. I don't care for the newspapers, so I don't read them. Indian current events don't interest me, you see, because whatever happens there has no real effect on the world. India is not in a position to affect the world. Although there is no sure way to divide up opinions into spiritual, political, or otherwise, you may call this a political opinion.

How can India give direction to or influence the world? India has neither the power nor the moral status. The spirituality you claim does not actually work in the life of the country. You have to show the world that the oneness of life you have preached for centuries operates in the daily life of this country, as well as in the lives of individuals. That is difficult.

No one is interested in what India says or does. It doesn't have the necessary stature to affect world events. The only thing about India that interests the rest of the world is the question,

'What will happen to her millions and millions of people? In which direction, towards what camp, is she going to move?'

Marxism as a religion has failed. Even Maoism is dead. Even the Marxist countries are looking for a new God now. They have lost faith in man and are once again looking for new God, new Church, new Bible, a new priest. The search is on for a different kind of freedom.

The only difference between east and west is the difference in our religions. Christianity has not produced such weird characters as we have in this country. Here religion is an individual affair. Each one has set up his own shop and is selling his particular wares. That's why we have the variety here, which is lacking in the west. This variety is the most attractive part of our so-called religious heritage.

Hinduism is not religion. It is a combination and confusion of many things. The actual word '*Hindu*' comes from a lost non-*Sanskrit* word, no longer in use. You wouldn't know anything about it. The invading Aryans who set up the *Brahmanic* social structure found native Indians to have dark complexion and called their religion the religion of the black - '*Hindu*'. The scholars and *pundits* may not like my interpretation, but it is correct and historical. Again, I repeat Hinduism is not a religion in the usual sense; it is like a street with hundreds of shops…Rajneesh's sex shop next to J. Krishnamurti's awareness shop, which is next to Maharshi's meditation shop, which is next door to Sai Baba's magic shop, which is next to… Basically they are all the same, exactly the same. Each claims that his wares are the best to be found in the market. Some products, like Pears Soap, have been in the market so long that people have come to know, depend upon them, and consider them superior to others. The durability of a particular product doesn't mean very much.

Everything in this country is entertainment. The politicians thrive on the gullibility of men. Religions thrive on the credulity of others. Well, we are damn fools, you see. That's all there is to it.

I don't think anything better will happen *to* man, or *for* man. It is because of the industrial revolution that far-reaching changes are sweeping the world. Nations like Russia, America, and other western nations, have taken advantage of the industrial revolution to push technology ahead. How effective these changes will be is anybody's guess. The regime of science and technology is already slipping...

'Progress' means 'to advance into enemy territory'. You are hopeful that unbridled progress will bring a solution to our problems. If it was that clear-cut, we might as well program the computers and see what they have to say regarding our future and our destinies. But this will give us no guarantee as to where the future will lead.

Something expected and unpredictable happens and the whole course is suddenly changed. We take it for granted that we can channel life in the direction we want, but there is no guarantee we will succeed. Events are really independent of one another. We create and put them together. We have created the philosophical structure of thought, but that does not mean that there is a pattern or purpose for everything. Nor does it mean that everything is predetermined.

Man has always lived in hope and will probably die in hope. In the light of the tremendous destructive power he now has at his command, he will probably take every other form of life with him when he goes.

This is not my doomsday song, but when you look realistically at our situation this seems to be the lot of us all, like it or not. You are mistaken if you think or hope that we can put the whole momentum of human history on a different track. We need to be saved from those saviours who promise the millennium just around the corner.

You see, to divide life between the material and the spiritual has absolutely no meaning to me. All this hogwash about the spiritual life is born out of the assumption that there is a spirit, which has an independent existence of its own. The assumption makes no sense. It's just a belief. It doesn't mean anything at all. I have no way of transmitting this certainty to you. There is nothing that will rise or reincarnate itself after I die. For you to speculate on the beyond has no meaning.

The demand for survival and the need to reproduce one's self is inherent in the nature of life. Your sexuality, your progeny, your family structure and so much more are an extension of this basic natural drive to survive and procreate.

If, when this body is buried, the memories people have of me are buried along with it; that will be the end of me. Very often people ask me, 'Are you not going to leave any instructions on how we should dispose of your dead body?' What the hell! Who wants to leave any instructions? It will begin to smell and become a nuisance to society... It's not my problem, but society's.

I don't have much contact with my family. They come and visit me sometimes. That's all. I have no emotional links with them, or with anybody for that matter. Not even with Valentine, the old Swiss lady I have been with for the last twenty years. I don't think I have any emotional link with anybody. I probably did not have even with my wife with whom I lived for twenty years. I really don't know what kind of links one should have.

What obsessed me most was to find out the answer to my question. It was the one overriding thing for me. What was *behind* the abstraction, these people, including J. Krishnamurti, were throwing at me? If there is nothing there, how could they have created all this mischief in the world? I understood that you could kid yourself and others, but I wanted an answer. I never got an answer; the question just burnt itself out.

That does not mean that I am enlightened, or that I know the Truth. Those who have claimed such things have fooled themselves and others. All of them are wrong. Not that I am superior to them or any such thing, but it is just that they are making claims that have no real basis at all. That was and is my certainty. There is no power in the world that can make me accept anything. So I am not in conflict with the power structure. I am not interested in taking anything away from anybody.

Whatever else I may or may not have been, I've never been a romantic in that sense. All that is romanticism for me. Romanticism is not my reality. Nothing has ever, or will ever, sweep me off my feet. It is not that I am the opposite of that, a man of reason. It is the element of reason in me that revolted against itself. I am not anti-rational or a-rational, just un-rational. You may infer a rational meaning in what I say or do, but it is *your* doing, not mine. I am not interested in anyone's search for happiness, romance, or escape...

There is no experience here, so how can there be these dramatic, crazy experiences? I have no way of separating myself from events; the event and I are one and the same. I'm sure you don't want me to say any crude things as far as sex is concerned. It's just a release of tension. I don't romanticize at all about this kind of stuff. As I once told my wife, 'Don't talk of love and intimacy to me: what keeps us together is sex. The problem is that I for some reason cannot have sex with another woman. That is my problem. I have no way of freeing myself from this problem.' I don't know if all this makes any sense to you. All this talk of love never meant anything to me. That's the end of this obsession with sex.

Yes, once I made love to another woman, but that was a situation not of my own making. I won't say I was seduced. It doesn't matter whether one seduces another or is himself seduced; the fact is you did it. It was not *that* person who was responsible.

It was a peculiar kind of auto-eroticism that was involved in this case. I was *using* that person.

It is a terrible thing to use somebody to get pleasure. Whether you use an idea, a concept, a drug, or a person, or anything else, you cannot have pleasure without *using* something. This revolted me. I am not interested in using, influencing or changing anybody. This is a statement on what *I* am, how *I* lived, nothing more. This will not be of any tremendous value for mankind and should not be preserved for posterity. I don't believe in posterity. *I have no teaching*. There is *nothing* to preserve. Teaching implies something that can be used to bring about a change. Sorry... There is no teaching here, just disjointed, disconnected sentences. What is there is only your interpretation of either the written or spoken word, nothing else. The answers you get are yours. They are your property, not mine. For this reason there is not now, nor will there ever be, any kind of copyright for whatever I am saying. I have no claims.

My mother died when I was seven days old. My maternal grandparents took care of me. My grandfather was a Theosophist. He was a wealthy man and instilled a strong religious atmosphere around the house. So, in that sense, J Krishnamurti was also a part of my background. They had his picture on every wall; I could not avoid him. I did not go to him in search of anything. He was just part of my background; it would have been remarkable had I never gone to see him. My problem was to free myself from the whole background that was strangling me. That's all.

I grew up mostly in Madras, in the Theosophical Society. I went to the University of Madras. I lived most of my formative years with and amongst the Theosophists. From the very beginning, they repelled me in a way. But I continued to fend for myself. I wanted so much to free myself from my past. I tried *so* hard. After J Krishnamurti walked out on the whole thing I eventually broke from them also.

Annie Besant was a remarkable woman. I met her when I was fourteen. I remember her oratory. My grandfather was very close to Annie Besant. She was an institution. I think India has every reason to be thankful to her, in more respects than one. But the modern generation doesn't know a thing about her. Neither do they know much of Gandhi. It is difficult to see how much the people now remember about him. This new film on him will probably spark some interest in his life.

I never liked him for some reason or the other. Perhaps it was my Theosophical background. Above all, he was a mixture of saint and politician. I think he was the only man amongst the whole lot who really tried to model his life after what he professed to believe in. He may have failed – he *has* failed in my opinion – but the fact that he tried to live according to the model he had before him, made him an interesting chap. Many others besides him were instrumental in gaining India's freedom. What he has left this country is nothing. It is a sentimental thing to give lectures on him every year on his birthday.

You cannot exonerate the founders and leaders of religions. The teachings of all those teachers and saviours of mankind have resulted in only violence. Everybody talked of peace and love, while their followers practised violence.

There is something funny about the whole business. It was this gap between word and deed that signalled to me early on that something was very wrong. I felt that the teachings were wrong, but lacked certainty. I had no way of brushing them aside; putting them entirely out of my consciousness. I was not ready to accept any of it on sentimental grounds. Even when my efforts to be rid of it resulted in episodes of Christ and Buddha consciousness, still I was discontent. I knew that there *must* be something wrong somewhere. This was really my problem, you know.

It is like the man who is riding a tiger and is thrown off. The tiger, maintaining its own momentum, continues on – it's gone.

That's all there is to it. You cannot do anything with the tiger any more. So you never again have the fear of encountering or riding the tiger. It is finished. It has gone.

So I think there is little point in my doing anything in the society – it has its own momentum. Anything you try to do will engulf you and add to that momentum. Who has given the mandate to all these people to save mankind? Compassion and love are two of their gimmicks.

Leadbeater was also part of my background. He never impressed me very much. I am aware that there were rumours that he was a homosexual. It doesn't matter to me; sex is a part of life. Homosexuality, lesbianism, heterosexuality, it's all the same. I don't have any moral position. Society, which has created all these sociopaths, has invented morality to protect itself from them. Count me out. Society has created the 'saints and sinners'. I don't accept them such.

There can be error, mistakes, weakness, but no sin for me. I personally see no reason why we should bother with the Bible, *Koran*, or the *Gita*, or the *Dhammapada*. We have a political body with its civil and criminal codes; that should be sufficient to handle the problem.

It's Terror, Not Love, That Keeps Us Together

The biological instinct is very powerful, and the fear of extinction, not love and compassion, will probably be the saviour of mankind.

When I use the term 'natural state' it is not a synonym for 'enlightenment', 'freedom', or 'God-realization', and so forth. Not at all. When the totality of mankind's knowledge and experience loses its stranglehold on the body, the physical organism, then the body is allowed to function in its own harmonious way. Your natural state is a biological, neurological, and physical state.

I can make no definitive statements about the part genes play in the evolutionary process, but at the moment it appears that Darwin was at least partially wrong in insisting that acquired characteristics could not be genetically transmitted. I think that they are transmitted in some fashion. I am not competent enough to say whether the genes play any part in the transmission.

Anyway, the problem lies in our psyche. We function in a thought-sphere, and not in our biology. The separative thought structure, which is the totality of man's thoughts, feelings, experiences, and so on – what we call psyche or soul or self is creating the disturbance. That is what is responsible for our misery; that's what continues the battle that is going on there [in the human being] all the time. This interloper, the thought sphere, has created your entire value system. The body is not in the least interested in values, much less a value system. It is only concerned with intelligent moment-to-moment survival, and nothing else. Spiritual 'values' have no meaning to it. When, through some miracle or chance, you are freed from the hold of thought and culture, you are left with the body's natural functions, and nothing else. It then functions without the interference of thought. Unfortunately, the servant, which is the thought structure that is there, has taken possession of the house. But he can no longer control and run the household. So he must be dislodged. It is in this sense that I use the term 'natural state', without any connotation of spirituality or enlightenment.

Nature does not use models. No two leaves are the same; no two human beings are the same. I understand your problem. You are not the first scientist demanding 'scientific proof', throwing questions at me like, "Why can't we test these statements you are making". First of all, I am not selling anything. Second, their interest and yours, is to use this natural state in your misguided efforts to change or 'save' mankind. I say that no change is necessary, period. Your corrupt society has put into you this notion of change, that you are this and you must be that. Anything that insists that you be something other than what you in fact are is the very thing that is falsifying you and the world. I somehow stumbled into this natural state on my own, and I cannot, under any circumstances transmit it to others. It has no social, political, commercial, or transformational value to anyone.

I do not sit upon platforms haranguing you, demanding that you change the world. As things are, you and the world – which are not two separate things – cannot be any different. All these attempts on the part of man to change himself go entirely against the way nature is operating. That is why I am not interested. Sorry! Take it or leave it. It's up to you. Whether you praise me or insult me I am not in the least interested. It is your affair. I don't fit into the picture [of 'scientific investigation'] at all. I am only talking about it in response to your questions. You throw the ball, and it bounces back. There is no urge in me to express myself to you or anyone else.

Culture is a way of life and the way of thinking of a people. To me, this is culture: how we entertain ourselves, how we speculate about reality, what kind of things we are interested in, what kind of art we have, so on. Whether the culture is Oriental or Occidental, it is basically the same. I don't see any difference between the two except one of accent, just as we all speak English with different accents. All human beings are exactly the same, whether they are Russian, American or Indian. What is going on in the head of that man walking in the street is no different from what is going on inside the head of a person walking in a street in New York. Basically it is the same. His goal may be different. But the instrument he is using to achieve his goal is exactly the same, namely, his trying to become something other than what he is.

I am not interested in helping anyone... Things have gone too far. If, just to take one example, the evermore-sophisticated genetic engineering techniques are monopolized by the state, we are sunk. What little freedom is still open to mankind will be brought under the control of the state, and the state will be in a position to create designer human beings, any type it wants, with impunity. It is all very respectable. Mankind will be robotized on a scale never dreamt before. What can be done to stop or prevent that sort of catastrophe? I say, nothing. It is too late. You may call me a sceptic, a cynic, a this or a that, but this is hard realism. It is your privilege to think what you will, but I fail to see any way out, as long as man remains as he is, which is almost a certainty. I don't see how it is possible for us to reverse this trend.

This crisis has not arrived unannounced. It has been building up for a long time, from the day man felt this self-consciousness in himself, and decided that the world was created for him to hold and rule. On that day he laid the foundation for the total destruction of everything that nature has taken so many millennia to create and build.

There is a process – I wouldn't necessarily call it evolution – but when it slows down then a revolution takes place. Nature tries to put together something and start all over again, just for the sake of creating. This is the only true creativity. Nature uses no models or precedents, and so has nothing to do with art per se.

Artists find it comforting to think that they are creative: 'creative art', 'creative ideas', and 'creative politics'. It's nonsense. There is nothing really creative in them in the sense of doing anything original, new or free. The artists pick something here and something there, put them together, and think they have created something marvellous. They are using something that is already there; their work is an imitation. Only, they are not decorous enough to admit that. They are all imitating something that is already there. Imitation and style are the only 'creativity' we have. We each have our own style according to the school we attended, the language we are taught, the books we have read, and the examinations we have taken. And within that framework again we each have our own style. Perfecting style and technique is all that operates there.

The framing of what there is by the mind is what you call beauty. Beauty is [in] the frame[ing]. The framing creates the conclusion, the thought, which it then calls beauty. Otherwise there is no beauty at all. Beauty is not in the object. Nor is it in the eye of the beholder. To say, like the Upanishads do, that the total absence of the self is beauty is a lot of hogwash! The act of capturing and framing, which thought creates for us, is what we call beauty. Perhaps I am going off on a tangent...

You want to make something of what I am saying, to use it somehow to further your own aims. You may say that it is for humanity's sake, but really you don't give a damn about society at all. What I am saying cannot possibly be of any use to you or your society. It can only put an end to you as you know yourself now.

Neither is what I am saying of any use to me because I cannot set up any holy business and make money. It is just impossible for me. I am not interested in freeing anyone or taking anybody from his or her gurus. You can go to the temples and pray there. You certainly get some comfort. You need to be comforted: that is what you want. And they provide you with that. This is a wrong place to come. Go anywhere you want. I have no interest in freeing you at all. I don't even believe in altering you in any way, or saving or reforming society, or doing anything for mankind.

It is the constant demand for permanence that cripples the society. Because we all seek permanence inwardly, we demand that those things, which we perceive to lie outside ourselves, society, humanity, the nation, and the world also be permanent. We seek our permanence through them. All forms of permanence, whether personal or collective, are your own creation. They are all an extension of the very same demand for permanence. But nothing is permanent. Our efforts to make things permanent go entirely against the way of nature. Somehow you know that you will not succeed in your demand for permanence. Yet you persist.

Life is something, which you cannot capture, contain, and give expression to. Energy is an expression of life. What is death? It is simply a condition of the human body. There is no such thing as death. What you have are ideas about death, ideas that arise when you sense the absence of another person. Your own death, or the death of your near and dear ones, is not something you can experience. What you actually experience is the void created by the disappearance of another individual, and the unsatisfied demand to maintain the continuity of your relationship with that person for a non-existent eternity. The arena for the continuation of all these 'permanent' relationships is the tomorrow, heaven, next life, and so on. These things are the inventions of a mind interested only in its undisturbed, permanent continuity in a 'self'-generated, fictitious future. The basic method of maintaining the continuity is the incessant repetition of the question, "How? How? How?" "How am I to live? How can I be happy? How can I be sure I will be happy tomorrow?" This has made life an insoluble dilemma for us. We want to know, and through that knowledge we hope to continue on with our miserable existences forever.

Society cannot be interested in what I am talking about. Society is, after all, two individuals or a thousand of them put together. Because I am a direct threat to you individually as you know and experience yourself I am also a threat to society. How can society possibly be interested in this sort of thing? Not a chance. Society is the sum of relationships, and despite what you may find agreeable to believe, all these relationships are sordid and horrible. This is the unsavoury fact; take it or live it. You cannot help but superimpose over these horrible ugly relationships a soothing fictitious veneer of "loving", "compassionate", "brotherly", and "harmonious" or some other fancy relationships.

All this talk of "here and now", much less a "here and now" within which can solve all your miseries, is, for me, pure bunk. All you know is separateness and duration, space and time, which is the 'frame' superimposed by the mind over the flow of life. But anything that happens in space and time is limiting the energy of life. What life is I don't know; nor will I ever. You can say that life is this, that, or the other, and give hundreds of definitions. But the definitions do not capture life. It's like a flowing river. You take a bucket full of water from it, analyze it into its constituent elements, and say that the river is the same [as the bucketful of water]. But the quality of flow is absent in the water in the bucket. So, as the Zen proverb says: "You can never cross the same river twice". It's flowing all the time.

You cannot talk of life or of death because life has no beginning or end, period. You can say there is life because you are responding to stimuli. But what happens after you are dead? The word 'dead' is only a definition, a condition of your body. The body itself, after what is called clinical death, no longer responds to stimuli the way in which we know it now. It is probably still responding in some fashion: the brain waves continue for a long time after clinical death takes place.

Through your death you are giving continuity to life, or whatever you call it. I can't say you are dead: only that you are not useful to me anymore. If you bury a dead body, something is happening there; if you burn the body, the ashes are enriching the soil; if you throw it in water, the fish will eat it; if you leave it there in the vulture-pit, the vultures will eat it. You are providing the means for the continuity of life.

So, you can't say the body is dead. It is not metaphysics that I am talking about here. It is only your fear of something coming to an end that is the problem. Do you want to be free from that fear? I say, "No." The ending of fear is the ending of you, as you know yourself. I am not talking of the psychological, romantic death of "dying to your yesterdays". That body of yours, I assure you, drops dead on the spot the moment the continuity of knowledge is broken.

All you are interested in as a scientist is self-fulfilment, the ultimate goal of a Nobel Prize, and power. I am very sorry. Personally, you may not be interested in that kind of thing. That's all. I encourage that kind of pursuit. Of course, you scientists have made all this comfort-bearing technology possible, and in that sense, I, like all those who enjoy the benefits of modern technology, am indeed indebted. I don't want to go back to the days of the spinning wheel and the bullock cart. That would be too silly, too absurd. Pure science is nothing but speculation. The scientists discuss formulas endlessly and provide us with some equations. But I am not at all taken in by the "march of progress" and all that rot. The first trip I made to the U.S. in the thirties took more than a full day; we had to stop everywhere. Later, the same trip took eighteen hours, then twelve hours, and even more recently six hours and three, and so on. And if the supersonic jets are put to commercial use we may be able to make the trip in one-and-a-half hours.

All right, that's progress. But the same technology that makes fast international travel possible is making ever more deadly military fighter planes. How many of these planes are we using for faster and more comfortable travel from one point to another? And how many more hundreds of planes are we using to destroy life and property? You call this progress? I don't know. As the comforts increase, we come to depend upon them, and are loath to give up anything we have.

Within a particular frame I say it is progress. I am now living in an air-conditioned room. My grandfather used a servant who sat in the hot sun and pulled the *pankha*, and before that we used a palm leaf hand fan. As we move in to more and more comfortable situations we don't want to give up anything.

Why do you expect others to give up all they have? The poor man there is not ready to give up his tiny little hut, and you expect all the rich men to give up all their mansions. No, they are just not going to do that. They will fight to their last breath to protect what they have, and kill themselves in the process. That is inevitable. What do wild animals do? They at first try to flee, then fight until they kill each other.

There is no such thing as knowledge for knowledge's sake or art for art's sake. It is certainly not for the benefit of mankind. Knowledge gives me power: "I know and you don't know".

I may be wrong, but I feel that man's problems, even his psychological problems, can only be solved through the help of his genes. If they can show that the tendency, say, to steal, is genetically determined, where will that leave us? It implies that man has no freedom of action in any area. Even the capacity to learn a language is also genetically determined. The genes control the whole thing; every tendency, capacity, and kind of behaviour.

Man has no freedom of action. His wanting and demanding freedom of action seems to be the cause of his suffering. I am not at all proposing the fatalistic philosophy that people preach in this country. My emphasis is quite different.

Whether you like it or not, they are going to do aggressive research in the field of genetics. You have no say in the matter. If you don't do it someone else will. How can you stop it? Any schoolboy knows how they make an atom bomb. And on a worldwide basis, huge amount of fissionable materials are already missing. They will end up in God-knows-whose hands. The know-how is available to everyone. One day someone is going to use it. Then we will be in trouble. If you don't do it [the research], because you are prevented by some ethical code, it's not going to work, because the code won't prevent someone else.

Postpone the evil day? Is that it? That's all we are trying to do. But for whose benefit? I am not singing a gloomy song of doom. If mankind goes, I am ready to go with it. But what can we do about it? There isn't a thing we can do. It is too far-gone.

I don't think that we deliberately took the wrong path. Something happened long ago to the human race. We are now a menace to the planet. Perhaps it is nature's way to clear away and start afresh in the fastest way. I don't see any scheme in nature, do you? We project our own ideations and mentations on to nature and imagine it to be sweetly ordered. We imagine that there is a scheme or plan, and such a thing as evolution. I don't see any such thing. There may be no evolution except what we see in nature and what we project onto it. By putting things together we surmise that that has evolved from this.

Somewhere along the line the process slows down. And when it does, then it takes a leap. This we call a mutation. Is there any relation between the two? Seeking to find a scheme behind it all, we link up these two things and call it evolution. It is the same in physics.

So, what do we do? I don't have the answer. It is not given to me. No one has chosen or elected me to be the saviour of mankind. All this talk of a permanent, eternal, perfect mankind has absolutely no meaning to me. I am interested only in the way we are functioning right now.

It [the body] is not thinking in terms of a hundred years, or two hundred years, or even tomorrow. No, it is only interested in survival now. If it is confronted with danger, it throws in everything it has, that is, all its resources, to survive in that particular situation. If it survives that moment, then the next moment is there for it. That is its own reward: to go on living for one more moment. This is the way the body is functioning now. Don't bother inventing philosophies of the moment, situational models, and all that. The body functions from moment to moment because the sensory perceptions and responses to the stimuli are also from moment to moment. Each perception or response is independent. What the purpose of the body is, why it is there, where it all may be heading, I really don't know. I have no way of finding out. If you think you know, then good luck to you! So, why bother trying to stop the growth of genetic engineering?

So, what is the motivation behind all this research? Tell me. The healthy pursuit of knowledge, for the satisfaction of curiosity…? But it doesn't stop there. Its exploited… And I am afraid you cannot so easily exonerate the scientists themselves. Einstein encouraged Roosevelt to drop the atom bomb. "If you don't do it, they will", he said. Out of his contempt for Germany and gratitude to the United States, which helped him flourish in his work and produce tremendous results, he gave that advice. He came to regret that advice later on. That doesn't matter.

Don't you think that pollution goes hand in hand with your research? Where do you draw the line? These environmental problems have been allowed to escalate into huge crises, so huge that in fact they are beyond what any individual or even ecologists can tackle any more. Look out of the window. Observe the sickening fumes, the poisonous air. The factories are pumping out millions of tons, of deadly wastes. There is more pollution here than in Western countries. To clean up the exhaust fumes from all the contaminating chemicals takes huge amounts of money. These companies are not going to voluntarily clean up the mess. Do you think General Motors and the others give a damn? If I had any shares in a company, and I don't actually, I would want dividends, not a bill for clean-up costs. Any management team that advocated corporate responsibility would be run out of office at once. As a shareholder I would want income, period. I wouldn't give a damn for all the people, animals, and plants that are there.

Now it has become fashionable to become an ecologist. Prince Philip's talk of saving the whales is a joke to me. And Queen Anne talks of saving the seals! Why are they concerned about whales and seals? If what I read is true, only fifteen percent of all the animal species that ever lived are alive today. All the other species have become extinct. Only five percent of all the plant species that ever existed exist now. So, extinction of species is the regular order of things in nature. Perhaps man should have become extinct long ago. I don't know. It's too late now. This one species alone is increasing the rate of extinction of all other species beyond what could have been thought possible. The self-consciousness in the human species, the idea that the world was created for man alone, is the real problem. The useless ecologists, form groups, attend meetings, collect funds, start foundations, build organizations worth millions with presidents and vice-presidents, and they all make money. It may sound very cynical to you, but the fact of the matter is that they have no real power. The solutions do not lie with them. The problem is out of their hands. Governments have the power to do something, but they are not interested.

You may call me a cynic, but the cynic is a realist who has

his feet firmly planted in the ground. You don't want to look at the reality of the situation. I still maintain that it is not love, compassion, humanism, or brotherly sentiments that will save mankind. No, not at all. It is the sheer terror of extinction that can save us, if anything can. Each cell of a living organism cooperates with the cell next to it. It does not need any sentiment or declarations of undying love to do so. Each cell is wise enough to know that if its neighbour goes, it also goes. The cells stick together not out of brotherhood, love and that kind of thing, but out of the urgent drive to survive.

It is the same with us, but only in a larger scale. Soon we will all come to know one simple thing: if I try to destroy you, I will also be destroyed. We see the superpowers of today signing arms control pacts, rushing to sign no-first-strike accords, and the like. Even the big bully boys, who have among them controlled the world's resources, no longer talk about a winnable nuclear war. Even the arrogant, swashbuckling United States has changed its tune. It no longer talks – as it did twenty years ago under Dulles and other cold warriors – of massive retaliation. If you read the Time magazine now, it doesn't talk about the United States as the mightiest, the richest, the most powerful, and the most invincible of all nations. It refers to it as "one of the superpowers".

If America were on the losing side in a big war, then what it would do is anybody's guess. I am not personally alarmed or concerned at all: if the Americans want to blow up the world, I am ready to go with them and with the rest of the world. But that's not the point. I am reasonably convinced that the Russians won't blow up the world. They have already suffered so much: they know first-hand the horrors of war. They were invaded and they lost twenty-million of their citizens, while Americans lost few lives, gained immense power as a result of the war, and sacrificed only some of its natural resources. Hitler created full employment in the U.S. overnight.

America showered bombs on the poor Vietnamese at a cost of $101 billion. It is that war that shattered the dollar. Each time that Vietnamese fellow walking in flip-flops brought down with his Tommy gun planes worth millions and millions of dollars, it was not just the paper greenback money that was lost, but also all those material resources of the earth.

Here in India it is the same story. We still call this a non-violent nation! It's a joke to me. You scientists are the ones who control the fate of the world, not these gurus, not these religious people. The fate of the world is in your hands and not in the hands of government. But your research funds have to come from them. They hold the strings. So, what do we do? The situation is so horrible. What do we do? I want to know. But still we play with each other: "Who has an edge over whom in the world?"

The chap who planted the tree is not going to eat its fruit. Some future generations are going to enjoy it. You think it's the same thing, because you feel good about the continuity you will have with them. I am not saying anything against it. Lay the roads, dig the tunnels and all that for future generations... I am only pointing out that there may not be anyone left to enjoy all those fine things!

There is nothing wrong about it. I am on your side. Do what you have to, but don't conveniently place it under the fabric of humanitarianism, brotherly love, self-sacrifice, and such other comforting ideas. At the same time, I am telling you that the fate of the planet is in the hands of today's scientists, not in the hands of the mystics and holy men, who come talking of changing the world, of creating a heaven on earth. It is these ideas, full of absolute and poetic fancy, that have turned this place into a hell. I have entrusted the whole thing to the scientists.

I have more faith in you and your colleagues than in all these people that are going around 'saving' mankind. We need to be saved from the self-appointed saviours of mankind. They are the ones who are responsible for the terrible situation we find ourselves in today. We don't realize that it is they who have created this mess for us. They had their day, and have utterly, totally failed. Still they refuse to take a back seat. That's it. We are stuck. You study the history of mankind: monarchies, revolutions, democracies, and more revolutions. Everything has failed us; everything is over. Not one ideology will survive. What's left for us? Democracy, the 'noble experiment', is over. Everything is over. We find ourselves in a situation where your boss will decide these issues.

Take the problem of starvation. One side says, "My political system will solve the problem of starvation in this world", and the other side says, "No, mine will"; and both of them end up on the battlefield brandishing their atomic weapons. That is the reality of the situation. Everywhere, on every continent, there is confrontation.

The basic issue in the world is, of course, economic: who will control the resources of this world? The nine rich nations of the world have been so used to controlling the resources of the world. They sit in Basel, Switzerland, and say, "Here is the price you must take for your products. Take it or leave it". A country like United States may talk of freedom, democracy, and justice, but they would like to have military governments in countries like those of South America. They prefer to do business with militarized, authoritarian states. A military general is very useful to run those countries. That is a fact.

Who or what can save you from all this? Not I, you may be sure. I am not a saviour of mankind. I don't even want to save you. You can stay in heaven or hell as the case may be… The fact is you already are in hell, and seem to enjoy it. Good luck to you!

As an individual you can help. But the moment you start an institution, and the institutions try to enlist individuals' help, and then the whole thing is destroyed. You have to organize, and there is no other way. That means my plan and your plan. It means war. Look at Mother Teresa. What is going on there? As an individual, she did a tremendous amount of service. But now she is only interested in the money, meeting the heads of governments and collecting money everywhere.

What you do is really an expression of your urge for self-fulfilment. You may not agree. What is it that you are trying to do there? You say your actions are very noble, meant to help the suffering world. Not a chance. You are only interested in your Nobel Prize, and the recognition it brings. How are you going to solve individually these immense problems of the world? Only through governments. There is no other way. And they are at each other's throat and armed to the teeth. Individually there isn't anything that you can do. Not a damn thing! You have so many conventions of scientists. What do they say?

Doing something collectively means war... It's like the European Economic Community. Each one has their own idea of running their country. Each country wants its own language, its own laws, its own king or queen, and resents any interference in its affairs from other countries. They have however; set aside these differences in order to solve larger problems. But individually what can you do? Why are you concerned about humanity?

We translate empathy as sadness, and the tears follow as a sentimental effect. But the tear ducts are there to protect your eyes from going blind, to keep them lubricated and cleansed, and not to respond to the suffering of others. This may be a crude way of putting things, but that's the fact of the matter.

The ethical considerations are what are standing in the way of your doing something. You don't have the energy to deal with this problem because you are throwing away what energy you do have by including in all these pointless ethical considerations. Otherwise you would find some way of neutralizing the whole thing. There must be some way of doing it. The superpowers will soon be humbled, neutralized in no time, by a single terrorist. Gaddaffi needs only one atomic hand grenade to neutralize the power of the mighty nations. They say that they already have a hand grenade that can blow up the Golden Gate Bridge. I wouldn't know. We now have hydrogen bombs, gas warfare, horrible weapons at our disposal. Look at the billions being poured into these arms. Even worse than the atomic grenades is the biological warfare. It's terrible. They have those atom bombs piling up. Yet they have no use for them. What huge amounts of money we are pouring into that! What for?

To me the question of whether God exists or not is irrelevant and immaterial. We have no use for God. We have used God to justify the killing of millions and millions of people. We exploit God. That's the positive aspect of it, not the negative. In the name of God we have killed more people than in the two world wars put together. In Japan millions of people died in the name of the sacred Buddha. Here in India, five thousand Jains were massacred in a single day. This is not a peaceful nation! You don't want to read your own history: it's full of violence from the beginning to the end.

The fear of extinction will probably bring us together, not 'love' or feeling of brotherhood. The invention of God, along with all those other beliefs, may have served mankind's instinct to survive for some time in the past, but not now. It's the extension of the same survival mechanism that now operates through the fear of extinction. The biological instinct is very powerful, and the fear of extinction, not love and compassion, will probably be the saviour of mankind.

4.

TRUTH

There is no such thing as truth...

➤   Throw Away Your Crutches

➤   Seeking Strengthens Separation

➤   What Kind Of A Human Being Do You Want?

Throw Away Your Crutches

If humanity is to be saved from the chaos of its own making, it has to be freed from the saviours of mankind.

You may not agree with me but when we talk about 'the quest for happiness', it is no different from any other sensual activity. As the matter of fact, all experiences, however extraordinary they may be, are in the area of sensuality. That is one major problem that we are facing today. Somewhere along the line, the human species experienced this self-consciousness for the first time. And it separated the human species from the rest of the species on this planet.

I don't even know if there is any such thing as evolution, but we are made to believe that there is such a thing. And it was at that time perhaps that thought took its birth. But thought in its birth, in its origin, in its content, in its expression, and in its action is very fascist. When I use the word 'fascist' I use it not in the political sense but to mean that thought controls and shapes our thinking and our actions. So it is a very protective mechanism. It has no doubt helped us to be what we are today. It has helped us to create our technology. It has made our life very comfortable. It has also made it possible for us to discover the laws of nature. But thought is a very protective mechanism and is interested in its own survival. At the same time thought is opposed fundamentally to the functioning of this living organism.

We are made to believe that there is such a thing as mind. But there is no such thing as your mind or my mind. Society or culture, or whatever you want to call it, has created us solely and wholly for the purpose of maintaining its own continuity and status quo. At the same time, it has also created the idea that there is such a thing as individual. But actually, there is a conflict between the two – the idea of the individual and the impossibility of functioning as an individual separate and distinct from the totality of man's thoughts and experiences.

Here at this point, I would like to emphasize that thoughts are not self-generated and spontaneous. I would even go one step further and ask, "Is there any such thing as thought?" The very question arises because we assume that there is such a thing as thought, and that we can separate ourselves from thought and look at it. But when we look at what we call thought, what we see is *about* thought and *not* thought itself. "What is thought?" The question arises only because of the assumption that there is such a thing as thought.

We use what we call thought to achieve our spiritual or material goals. We may consider the spiritual goals as 'higher'. The culture in which we are functioning places spiritual goals on a higher level than the materialistic goals. But the instrument that we are using is matter, which is thought. Thought to me is matter. Therefore, all our spiritual goals are materialistic in their value. And this is the conflict that is going on here. In this process, the totality of man's experiences created what we call a separate identity and a separate mind. But actually, if you want to experience anything, be it your own body, or your own experiences, you have no way of experiencing them without the use of knowledge that is passed on to you. In other words, I would say that thought is memory. Everything that is born out of thought is destructive. Anything that we discover, the laws of nature or whatever you call it, is used by us only for destructive purposes. And it is true that we have discovered quite a few of nature's laws, and the theories are constantly changing...

Thought is not the instrument for achieving anything other than the goals set before us by our culture or society, or whatever you want to call it. The basic problem we have to face today is this; the cultural input, or what society has placed before us as the goal for all of us to reach and attain, is the enemy of this living organism. Thought can only create problems; it cannot help us to solve any.

What I am talking about is not a thoughtless state. Even the invention of what is called a 'thoughtless state', placed before us by many spiritual teachers as a goal to be reached, is created by thought so that it can, by pursuing what it calls a thoughtless state, maintain its own continuity. So, whatever we experience in this process of achieving the goal of a thoughtless state strengthens and fortifies the very thing that we are trying to be free from.

It is thought that has invented the idea of cause and effect. There may not be any such thing as a cause at all. Every event is an individual and independent event. We link up all these events and try to create a story of our lives. But actually, every event is an independent event. If we accept the fact that every event is an independent event in our lives, it creates a tremendous problem of maintaining what we call 'identity'. And identity is the most important factor in our lives. We are able to maintain this identity through the constant use of memory, which is also thought. This constant use of memory or identity, or whatever you call it, is consuming a tremendous amount of energy, and it leaves us with no energy to deal with the problems of our living. Is there is any way that we can free ourselves from the identity? As I said, thought can only create problems; it cannot help us to solve them. Through dialectical thinking about thinking itself we are only sharpening that instrument. All philosophies help us only to sharpen this instrument.

Thought is very essential for us to survive in this world. But it cannot help us in achieving the goals that we have placed before ourselves. The goals are unachievable through the help of thought. The quest for happiness is impossible because there is no such thing as permanent happiness. There are moments of happiness, and there are moments of unhappiness. But the demand to be in a permanent state of happiness is the enemy of this body. This body is interested in maintaining its sensitivity of the sensory perceptions and also the sensitivity of the nervous system. That is very essential for the survival of this body. If we use that instrument of thought for trying to achieve the impossible goal of permanent happiness, the sensitivity of this body is destroyed. Therefore, the body is rejecting all that we are interested in – permanent happiness and permanent pleasure. So, we are not going to succeed in that attempt to be in a permanent state of happiness.

Through a repetitive process we are sharpening the intellect. But we are using tremendous amount of energy in this process. If the use of thought is limited to achieve only what we consider to be materialistic values and not our spiritual goals, what is it that is not possible for us in order to function sanely and intelligently. It does not mean that I am teaching a materialistic philosophy or any such thing. Thought is not intended for achieving spiritual goals or even to find out the significance, meaning, or purpose of life, or to be used for the quest for permanence or permanent pleasure.

I am not opposed to the theory of karma or reincarnation. But I am questioning the very foundation of the belief. There is reincarnation for those who believe in it, and there is no reincarnation for those who do not believe in it. But is there any such thing as reincarnation as a law of nature, like gravity and other laws of nature? My answer is "No". It doesn't matter whether you believe or not in reincarnation. If one is interested in finding out for himself and by himself, to resolve this problem of reincarnation, and get an answer for this oft-repeated question, "Is there such a thing as reincarnation?" you have to ask this fundamental question, "What is there now that you think will reincarnate?" Is there anything there? Is there any such thing as soul? Is there any such thing as the 'I'? Is there any such thing as the psyche? Whatever you see there, whatever you experience there is created only by the knowledge you have of that self. If you are lucky enough to be freed from the totality of knowledge, the knowledge of the self, reincarnation, and all kinds of things, then is it possible for you to experience any centre, any 'I', any self, any soul? So, to me the 'I' is nothing but a first-person singular pronoun, and I do not see any centre or Self there. So, the whole idea of reincarnation is built only on the foundation of our beliefs.

We have always been curious and interested in finding out why a child is born with deformities. And reincarnation was a very interesting theory evolved by the human mind at one time to explain *away* such situations and give us comfort in facing the situation that we have such people in our midst. But now it is possible for us, in the light of what they are doing in terms of genetic research and microbiology, to correct the deformities created by nature. Why should we want to attribute this misfortune to something terrible that we did in our previous life? That kind of belief comes in very handy to us. We have in our midst today a tremendous suffering, a tremendous amount of poverty, starvation, and degradation. It is very comforting for us to believe that, that suffering is there because the people who suffer did something terrible in their past life. That is no answer to give. That makes us take shelter in the belief and not do anything to solve the problem. The belief is neither spiritual nor human. In the name of doing something human to our fellow beings, we perpetrated inhuman deeds. The belief in reincarnation will only help us to look the other side and not to deal with the problem that is demanding answers from every thinking man in the world today.

think *guru* is the wrong word to use these days for all those spiritual gurus we have in the market, selling shoddy pieces of goods, and exploring the gullibility and credulity of people. A guru is one who tells you to throw away all the crutches that you have been made to believe are essential for your survival. The true guru tells you, "Throw them away, and don't replace them with the fancy crutches or even computerized crutches. You can walk; and if you fall, you will rise and walk again." Such is the man whom we consider, or even tradition considers, being the real guru, and not those who are selling those shoddy pieces of goods in the market place today. It is a business; it has become a holy business for people. I am not condemning anything. But as long as you depend upon somebody for solving your problems, so long you remain helpless. And this helplessness is exploited by the people who actually do not have the answers to your problems, but they give you some sort of a comforter. People are satisfied with these comforters and fall for this kind of thing, instead of dealing with the problems by themselves and for themselves.

You believe that the quest for happiness is all that anybody, whether he is a Russian, an American, an African, or an Indian, is interested in. I say that it is impossible to achieve such a goal because of the physical problem (of conflict with the body) that is involved in achieving that goal. It is assumed that the West is materialistic, and that it is looking towards the East for spiritual guidance. That is not really true. If you live for a longer period in the West, you will realize that those who are interested in these spiritual matters are not really the people who are guiding the destinies of this world. What is responsible for this sudden interest in spiritual matters and their looking to the East for succour is drugs. They gave them a new sort of experience. But they were not satisfied with repeating those experiences. They were looking around for varieties of religious experiences, whether they are from India, or from Japan or from China. They are attracted to these things because of the new language and new techniques.

The fact of the matter is that when once you have everything that you can reasonably ask for in this world, when all the material needs are taken care of, naturally the question arises, "Is that all?" When once you pose that question, "Is that all?" to yourself, you have created a tremendous market for this kind of business, the holy business. These people are exploiting the gullibility and credulity of the people, rather than helping them to resolve the basic problems, the human problems. It is not that simple. So we have to ask such questions over and over again. But all the questions we are asking are born out of the answers that we already have. It never occurs to us to ask why we keep asking the questions when we already have the answers given by the sages, saints, and saviours of mankind. We fail to realize that the answers that they have given us are the ones that are responsible for the tragedy of mankind. We don't question them. If we question the answers, we would be questioning the teachers. If humanity is to be saved from the chaos of its own making, it has to be freed from the saviours of mankind. That does not mean that you should destroy everything. You will have to ask questions not born out of the answers we already have. But is there any answer? That is all. There it stops. And the solution is there for mankind.

Seeking Strengthens Separation

The demand for change springs from self-consciousness, the separation from the singleness of the whole nature around us.

You are the medium through which I can express myself. There is no other way. I don't even have the impetus to express myself. You may very well ask me, "Why the hell do you talk? Why the hell do you meet people?" It is you who have brought all these people. Why do you ask me questions? That is one of the reasons why I have always avoided publicity of any kind. I don't want to promote myself, nor am I allowing others to promote me. I have no need to express myself at all. Not even the impetus to talk. I don't have it. He comes or she comes or you come. I am like a puppet sitting here. It's not just I; all of us are puppets. Nature is pulling the strings, but we believe that we are acting. If you function that way [as puppets], then the problems are simple. But we have superimposed on that [the idea of] a 'person' who is pulling those strings.

All of us are the same. That's what I am saying. I understand your problem. The actions of life are outside the field of thought. Life is simply a process of stimulus and response; and stimulus and response are one unitary movement. But it is thought that separates them and says that this is the response and that is the stimulus. Any action that is born out of thinking is destructive in its nature because thought is a self-perpetuating mechanism. Any action that is outside the field of thought is one continuous movement. It is one with the movement of life. It is that flow of things that I am referring to, you see. You don't even have to paddle out of the mainstream on to the banks there. But you are frightened of sinking in it.

To sidestep the complexities of this society is one of the biggest mistakes that we are making. But there is nothing out there, you see. All these godmen, gurus, and the flunkies (the most wicked word to use) are offering us a new oasis. You will find out that it is no different from other mirages. We are leaving everything for some mythical certainty offered to us. But this is the only reality and there is no other reality.

What I am emphasizing is, if your energy is not wasted in pursuit of some mythical certainties offered to you, life becomes very simple. But we end up being wasted, misled and misspent individuals. If that energy is released, what is it that we can't do to survive in the midst of these complexities of the world created by our culture? It is very simple. The attempt to sidestep these complexities is the very thing that is causing us all these problems.

Energy is something which cannot be defined and which cannot be understood. Not that I am mystifying it. The moment the dead thought tries to capture that energy, it [thought] is destroyed. Thought is matter. The moment it is created, it has to be destroyed. But that is the very thing that we resist, you see. Thought is born and is destroyed, and again it is born and again it is destroyed. The only way you can give continuity to thought is through this constant demand to experience everything. This is the only way you try to maintain the continuity of the 'experiencing structure'.

One thing that I emphasize all the time is that without knowledge you can't experience anything. What you do not know, you cannot experience. It is the knowledge that creates the experience, and it is the experience that strengthens the knowledge. At every moment of our existence, we have to know what is happening outside of us and what is happening inside of us. That is the only way you can maintain this continuity.

All these 'godmen' are giving you false comfort, and that is what people want. What I am saying is what the mainstream of population is interested in, either here or anywhere in the world. They hear what they want to hear. What I say is of no interest to them. If you say that God is redundant, it is not a rebellion against anything: you know religious thinking is outdated and outmoded. But I go one step further and say that all political ideologies are nothing but the warty outgrowth of the same religious thinking of man. They may call it a revolution. But revolution is only a revolution of things. You will only end up creating another value system, which may be slightly different from the value system that we want to destroy. But basically they are all the same. That is why when it [the revolution] settles down, it calls for another revolution. Even the talk of continuous revolution of Mao-Tse-Tung has failed. In the very nature of things, a revolution has to settle down.

I am questioning the very idea of consciousness. There is no such thing as consciousness at all. Consciousness is nothing but knowledge. Don't ask me how knowledge originated. Somewhere along the line knowledge started with you, and then you wanted to know about the things around. That is what I mean by 'self-consciousness'. You have become conscious of what is going on around you, and so naturally you want to know. What I am suggesting is that the very demand to understand the mystery of existence is destructive. Just leave the mystery alone.

What I am saying is not born out of my keen observation of things around me. It is not born out of logical thinking. It is not a logically ascertained premise. There was this makeup within me from the very beginning of rejecting everything totally. I lived amongst masterminds. They were not ordinary people. I have travelled everywhere, and, as I very often say, I was not born yesterday.

What I am saying is that this is something that you cannot totally reject through any volition or effort of yours. Somehow it happened to me. It is just a happening. It is acausal. The whole thing drained out of my system – the parameters that mankind has evolved, the thoughts, feelings and experiences throughout the ages. All this was thrown out of my system.

Why doesn't it happen to you? Well, the potential, the possibility is there, but the probability is zero. It is because you are all the time trying, and that is not letting what is there to express itself. Thought creates an armour all around itself. Any time a crack appears there, you patch it up…

Coming back to what I said earlier about rejecting the whole past, the experiences, thoughts and everything… It is not something that you can do through any effort, will or volition of yours. It's a miracle. So what I am emphasizing is that whatever has happened to me has happened despite everything I did. In fact, everything I did only blocked it. It prevented the possibility of whatever was there to express itself. Not that I have gained anything. Only what is there is able to express itself without any hindrance, without any constraints or restraints imposed on it by society for its own reasons, for its own continuity and stability.

The search is inevitable and is an integral part of it. That is why it has turned us all into neurotics and has created this duality for us. You see, ambition is a reality; competition is a reality. But you have superimposed on that reality the idea that you should not be ambitious. It has turned us all into neurotic individuals. We want two things at the same time.

Whether he is here or in America or in Russia or anywhere else, what does man want? He wants happiness without one moment of unhappiness. He wants permanent pleasure without pain. This is the basic demand – permanence. So it is this demand that has created the whole religious thinking – God, Truth or Reality. Since things in life are not permanent, we demand that there must be something permanent. That is why these religious teachers are peddling their wares in the streets. They offer you these comforts

– 'permanent happiness' or 'permanent bliss'. Are they ready to accept the fact that bliss, beatitude, immensity, love and compassion are also sensual?

This certainty that I have, is something that I cannot transmit to you. It does not mean that I will go and burn all the churches, temples, or bury all the Vedas etc, or that I will become a terrorist and mindlessly kill everyone. That's all too silly. It's neither 'love thy neighbour as thyself', nor the spiritual values, nor the human value system that can protect us from now on, but the terror that your very existence is at stake. You cannot survive unless the one that is next to you also survives. It's not cooperation on the basis of love and brotherhood, but it's the way this human body is functioning, the way that animals are functioning that can protect you. Animals do not kill their fellow beings (they are also beings, you see) for an ideology or for God.

You are not decent and decorous enough to admit that all your spiritual experiences – bliss, beatitude or love – are also sensual activities. Any activity of thought, whether it is called spiritual or sensual, is also a sensual activity. That's all that you are interested in. Your being in a blissful mood is a high, the do-gooder's high. You become a boy scout and take the lady across the road so that you can get some brownies. This is the do-gooder's high that they talk about. Jogging also gives you a high. Let's admit it.

The high is necessary for the survival of the experiencing structure, and not for this body. The body is rejecting all that. It doesn't want any of those things. The experiencing structure is separate and outside of us. You are trying to make everything part of the thought-sphere.

There is no individual. Where is the individual? You are not an individual. You are doing exactly the same thing that everybody is doing. Your feeling that you are an individual does not mean anything. The individual you are talking about is created by your culture. You are creating that non-existing individual there.

You are not separate from this body and that body. If you accept what I am talking about, it is a very dangerous situation. Your wife goes, you see. No relationship. Sorry... You don't want it! "How can you ask for this?" is all that I am saying. You are only trying to fit me into a framework by calling me an 'enlightened man'. This fellow here is telling everyone, "Jesus is living here. Why should I go to the Church?" He is crazy. Don't you think that they [the religious people] have all created a mess for us? They laid the foundation for the destruction.

You have not arrived anywhere. Even the claimants have not arrived anywhere. You don't have to reach for answers, because all the answers are really coming from the answers that you already have. But is there any way you can free yourself from that activity?

There is no other way I can point out the danger that is involved in your seeking whatever you are seeking. You see, there is this pleasure movement. I am not against the pleasure movement. I am neither preaching hedonism nor advocating any '-ism' or anything. What I am saying is a threat to 'you' as you know yourself and experience yourself. You necessarily have to fit me into that framework [of the Buddha, Jesus, and others], and if I don't succeed, you will say, "How can he be outside of it?" The way out for you is either to reject me totally, or to call me a fraud or a fake. You see, the feeling, "How can all of them be wrong?" prevents you from listening to me. Or else you put it another way and say that the content of whatever has happened to U.G. and to them is the same, but his expression is different.

I am not concerned about you at all. You can stay in hell, rot in hell, and do what you like. I am not here to save you. I don't mean you personally. What I am saying has no social content. I have opinions on everything in this world. You have your opinions, and I can also express opinions and judgements on everything. But my opinions and judgements are no more important than the opinions and judgements of your mother or that taxi driver there.

I was lecturing on the essential unity of all religions everywhere around the globe. But I haven't discovered anything. That's what's strange. I wanted moksha, what the Buddha had. Just the way you think about what I have or what Jesus Christ had. You see, the Buddha created U.G.; Jesus created Frank. You don't understand that, do you? You don't want this [U.G.] to go [out of your system], and that is the reason why you keep that [the Buddha, Christ, etc.] and perpetuate it. Both are the same. Culture has created the individual for the sole purpose of maintaining its continuity. Every time you condemn anger, that strengthens and fortifies the movement of your culture and your value system. Every time you praise the Lord, you are maintaining and perpetuating that self. Culture has created you and me for the sole purpose of maintaining its status quo. You don't want a change. You have invented something that is there today, and it will continue to be there after you are gone.

Many people want to fit me into traditional descriptions of things like Yoga. What happens is that the servant has taken possession of the running of the house in trying to influence everything there. Somehow, through some miracle he is forced to leave. When the servant leaves, he wants to adopt a scorched-earth policy. He wants to burn everything there. You want him to go but he won't go. He has become the master. So, this [your thought] is moving at a particular rhythm, at a particular tempo and speed. Suddenly when it stops, through no volition of yours, through no effort of yours, it blows up the whole thing here. That's all that has happened to me. From then on it [the organism] falls into a quiet natural rhythm and functions in its own way. That is why all those changes take place in the body.

The natural state is the functioning of this living organism. It is not a synonymous term for enlightenment or God-realization or self-realization. What is left here is this pulsating living organism. And the way it is functioning is no different from the mosquito that is sucking your blood.

It is not awareness. I don't like to use that word. It is not something that can be captured, contained and given expression to through your experiencing structure. It is outside the field of experience. So it cannot be shared with anyone. That's the reason why I am saying that he, you, or it, is the medium through which whatever I am saying is expressing itself. But you are distorting, correlating and garbling it. Thought cannot help doing that. When there is no path, where is the question of right or wrong? If you are making a path out of what I am saying, it is your tragedy. If you take another path, it is your misery.

I question the Big Bang theory. I am questioning even the fundamental particles. We will never be able to find the fundamental particles. I have mentioned the ionization of thought and an explosion. From then on, understanding is not through the instrument which we are using all the time to understand – the intellect. We have developed and sharpened the intellect through years. So, it [the intellect, in U.G.] understood in its own way that it is not the instrument, that there is no other instrument, and that there is nothing to understand. My problem was how to use this intellect to understand whatever I was looking for. But it didn't help me to understand a thing. So I was searching for some other instrument to understand, that is, intuition, this, that, and the other. But I realized that this is the only instrument I have; and the hope that I would understand something through some other instrument, on some other level, and some other way, disappeared. It dawned on me, "There is nothing to understand". When this happened, it hit me like a shaft of lightning. From then on, the very demand to understand anything was finished. That understanding is the one that is expressing itself now. And it cannot be used as an instrument to guide, direct or help me, you or anybody.

That explosion that occurred is happening all the time. It is all the time exploding. Any attempt on my part to understand anything at any given moment is exploded because that [thought] is the only instrument I have, and there is no other instrument. This instrument cannot invent a thing called hope again anymore. There is no hope of understanding. The moment it [thought] is forming something there, it is exploded, not through any volition, not through any effort, but that's exactly the way it happens. It is continuously happening all the time. That is the way life is moving along, it has no direction.

The body has no need to understand anything. The body does not have to learn anything, because anything you learn, anything you do is attempting to change, alter, shape or mould yourself into something better. This [body] is a perfect piece that has been created by nature. In this assemblage of the species of human beings on this planet, one being is endowed with the intelligence of an Einstein, another is endowed with the brawn of a Tyson and someone else is endowed with the beauty of a Marilyn Monroe. But two or three or all [of these characteristics] in one will be a great tragedy. I can't conceive any possibility of all the three blooming in one individual – brain, brawn, and beauty.

There is nothing to die here [in U.G.]. The body cannot be afraid of death. The movement that is created by society or culture is what does not want to come to an end. How it came to an end [in U.G.] I really don't know. What you are afraid of is not death. In fact, you don't want to be free from fear. Because when the fear comes to an end you will drop dead. That is its nature. It is the fear that makes you believe that you are living and that you will be dead. What we do not want is the fear to come to an end. That is why we have invented all these new minds, new science, new talk, therapies, choiceless awareness and various other gimmicks. Fear is the very thing that you do not want to be free from, what you call 'yourself' is fear. The 'you' is born out of fear; it lives in fear, functions in fear and dies in fear.

The body is not interested in dying... When the body encounters a cobra it steps back, and then you take a walk. The cobra is a marvellous creature. If you hurt it, you are hurting yourself. I mean it [hurting it] physically hurts you [back], not psychologically or romantically because it is all one movement of life. What I am saying is that you will never hurt that. The cooperation there springs from the total selfishness of mutual survival. It's like the cell in your body, which also can survive only when it cooperates with the cell next to it. Otherwise it has no chance of survival. That's the only way we can live together. But that has to percolate to the level of, if you want to use that word, your 'consciousness'. Only then you will live in this world peacefully. It is that total interdependence for survival on the physical level that can bring about unity. Only on that level.

The intellect is created by culture and is acquired. The intelligence that is necessary for survival is already there in the physical organism. You don't have to learn a thing. You need to be taught, you need to learn things only to survive in this world that we have created, the world of ideas. You need to know in order to survive. You have to fight for your share in the cake. Somebody comes along and says that you should fight without expecting any results. What the hell are you talking about? How can you act without expecting any results? As long as you live in this world you have to fight for your share. That is why they teach you, send you to school, and give you some tools. That is what society has done to you.

But religion comes along and tells you that you should fight for your share without expecting anything in return. That is why you are turned into a neurotic individual. Otherwise you will fight only for your share. You don't grab the whole thing. You grab the whole thing because you have been taught by religion, culture or something else to do so. Animals kill only for their survival and leave the rest of their game. You can call it garbage or whatever you want. Every other thing survives on that. If I take only whatever I need for myself, the rest is there for everybody. There won't be any shortage.

I won't say I am a misfit. I am part of the mainstream of life everywhere. At the same time, I have no roots anywhere. If I may put it that way, I am a rootless man of sorts. I have lived everywhere in this world, and I don't feel at home anywhere. It's very strange. I am one of the most travelled persons in this world. I have been travelling ever since I was fourteen, and since then I never lived in any place for more than six months at a time. My travelling is not born out of my compulsive need to travel. When people ask me, "Why do you travel?" I answer them, "Why do some birds travel from Siberia to a small bird sanctuary in Mysore State and then go back all the way?" I am like those migratory birds. It's very strange. I have travelled everywhere except in China.

I am quite satisfied with the world! Quite satisfied. The world cannot be any different. Travelling destroys many illusions and creates new illusions for us. I have discovered, to my dismay, if I may put it that way, that human nature is exactly the same whether a person is a Russian, or an American or someone from somewhere else. It is as though we all speak the same language, but the accent is different. I will probably speak [English] with an Andhra accent, you with a Kannada accent, and someone else with a French accent. But basically, human beings are exactly the same. There is absolutely no difference. I don't see any difference at all. Culture is probably responsible for the differences. We being what we are, the world cannot be any different. As long as there is a demand in you to bring about a change in yourself, you want to bring about a change in the world. Because you can't fit into the framework of culture and its value system, you want to change the world so that you can have a comfortable place in the world.

What makes you think that the world can be any different? Why do you want to change the world? All these utopias, all these ideas of creating a heaven on this earth are born out of the assumption that there is a heaven somewhere there and that we have to create that heaven on this planet. And that's the reason why we have turned this into a hell. You see, I don't call this a hell. I'd like to say it couldn't be any different.

Nature has provided us with tremendous wealth on this planet. If what they say is correct, twelve billion people can be fed with the resources that we already have on this planet. If eighty per cent of the people are underfed, then there is something wrong – something is wrong because we have cornered at one place all the resources of this world. I don't know. I am not competent enough to say, but they say that the Americans alone consume eighty per cent of this world's resources. What is it that is responsible for that?

The problem is this – nature has assembled all these species on this planet. The human species is no more important than any other species on this planet. For some reason, man accorded himself a superior place in this scheme of things. He thinks that he is created for some grander purpose than, if I could give a crude example, the mosquito that is sucking his blood. What is responsible for this is the value system that we have created. And the value system has come out of the religious thinking of man.

Man has created religion because it gives him a cover. This demand to fulfil himself, to seek something out there was made imperative because of this self-consciousness in you which occurred somewhere along the line of the evolutionary process. Man separated himself from the totality of nature. The religious thinking of man originated from the idols, gods, and spiritual teachers that we have created. So the whole trend is in the direction of creating a perfect man – without this you feel a kind of insecurity. You need something. That is why you have invented all this. You might as well take *Valium,* or use something, and forget about it. That [security] is all that you are interested in. And I don't want to run down the gurus and the godmen we are flooding the world with.

If seeking is part of nature, then why are you trying to change it? Why don't you accept it? You see, the problem is the demand to bring about a change. What is it that distinguishes us from animals? We think we are different, right? Thinking is responsible, and thinking is born out of this self-consciousness. When I use the word 'self-consciousness' I don't mean all that stuff we find in religious thinking. What I mean is very simple – I mean the feeling that you are different from the tape recorder there, that you are different from that blue door. This is what I mean by separation. That feeling doesn't exist in animals at all. We are made to believe that there is something that you can do, to bring about a change in and around you. The demand for change springs from this self-consciousness, the separation from the singleness of the whole nature around us.

Without separating yourself from the things around, you feel that you are unable to act. That's why I say that any action that is born out of your thinking, or let's say thought, is destructive. It is destroying the peace that is there. The way this living organism is functioning is marvellous. The human organism is a perfect specimen of the creation of nature. Nature is only interested in perfecting the species. But we have superimposed on that the idea of a perfect man, and that idea is the problem.

This idea is born out of the assumption that there is a perfect man like all these Buddhas, Jesuses, and others. You are trying to model your life after these great teachers. You want your behaviour patterns to be like theirs. But it's just not possible. A 'perfect being' does not exist at all. A perfect being is the end product of human culture, that is, the being we think as the perfect being. And you want everybody to be perfect that way. So going back to my point, nature's interest is only to create perfect species. It does not use any model. Every human being is something extraordinary and unique. If a being does not fit into the scheme of things, nature discards it and starts all over again.

Animals don't eat for pleasure. They eat for survival. Actually, whatever you project on animals is born out of your own ideation and mentations. It is born out of your subjectivist approach to the problem, which is also born out of your value system. Do we want to understand animals or the laws of nature with the idea of 'what do I get out of that'? Our desire to know the laws of nature is only to use them for perpetuating something here [in the human being]. So thought is, in its birth, in its content, in its expression, and also in its action, to use a very crude political word, fascist in nature. There is no way you can get away from that. It [thought] is a self-perpetuating mechanism.

We are operating under a value system, whether it is good or bad. You see, both good and bad, right and wrong, are not the reverse of a coin but are the same coin. They are like the two ends of the spectrum. One cannot exist independent of the other. When once you are finished with this duality, (I am using the word with much caution, although I don't like to use it) when you are no longer caught up in the dichotomy of right and wrong or good and bad, you can never do anything wrong. As long as you are caught up in it, the danger is that you will always do wrong; and if you don't do wrong, it is because you are a frightened 'chicken'. It is out of this cowardice that the whole religious thinking is born.

Anger is like an outburst of energy. It is like the high tide and the low tide in the sea. The problem is, "What to do with anger?" The question, "What to do with anger?" is something put in there by culture, because society considers an angry man a threat to its status quo, to its continuity.

I am not a threat. I am not a threat because I cannot, you see, conceive of the possibility of anything other than this. I am not interested in changing anything. You are the one that is all the time talking of bringing about a change. At the same time everything around you and inside of you is in a flux. It is constantly changing. Everything around you is changing; yet you don't want change. You see, that's the problem. Your unwillingness to change is really the problem, and you call it a tradition.

You and I are functioning in exactly the same way; and I am not anything that you are not. You think I am different from you. You have to take my word – at no time does the thought that I am different from you ever enter my mind. I know for certain that you are functioning in exactly the same way that I am functioning. But you are trying to channel the activity or movement of life both to get something and to maintain that continuity of what is put in there [in you] by culture. That is not the case here [in U.G.].

We think that thoughts are there inside of us. We think that they are self-generated and spontaneous. What is exactly there is what I call a thought-sphere. The thought-sphere is the totality of man's experiences, thoughts, and feelings passed on to us from generation to generation. In this context I want to mention that the brain is not a creator, but only a reactor. It is only reacting to stimuli. What you call thought is only the activity of the neurons in the brain. In other words, thought is memory. A stimulus activates the brain through the sensory perceptions and then brings memory into operation. It is nothing marvellous. It is just a computer with a lot of garbage put in there. So it is not a creator. The brain is not interested in solving any of the problems created by us. It is singularly incapable of dealing with the problems created by thought. Thought is outside and it is extraneous to the brain.

It is a very superficial division that we make between thought and instinct. Actually, there are no instincts in the human being at all. There is no such thing as instinct. That's all invented by your fanciful thinking. Thought processes are outside of you. Self-consciousness or separation [of ourselves] from the world around us occurs, they say (I am not competent enough to say anything) around the eighteenth month of the child. Until then the child cannot separate itself from whatever is happening there inside and outside of itself. But actually there is no inside and outside at all. What creates the inside and outside, or what creates the division between the inside and the outside is the movement of thought. Anything that is born out of thought is a self-protecting mechanism.

Nature uses the human species to destroy everything that it has created. Everything that is born out of thought, every discovery you have made so far is used for destructive purposes. Every invention of ours, every discovery of ours is pushing us in that direction of total annihilation of the human species.

Why does nature deliberately want to first create and then destroy? Because really nothing is ever born, and nothing ever dies. What has created the space between creation and destruction, or the time between the two, is thought. In nature there is no death or destruction at all. What occurs is the reshuffling of atoms. If there is a need or necessity to maintain the balance of energy in this universe, death occurs. You may not like it. We may condemn earthquakes. Surely they cause misery to so many thousands of people. And all this humanitarian activity around the world to send planeloads of supplies is really a commendable act. It helps those who are suffering there and those who have lost their properties. But it is the same kind of activity that is responsible for killing millions of people. What I am saying is that the destructive, war-making movement and the humanitarian movement on the other hand – both of them are born from the same source. In the long run, earthquakes and the eruption of volcanoes are part of nature's way of creating something new. Of course, I am not saying that you should not do anything in the way of helping those people.

The self-consciousness that occurred in the human species may be a necessary thing. I don't know. I am not claiming that I have a special insight into the workings of nature. You see for yourself. That's why I say that the very foundation of the human culture is to kill and to be killed. It has happened so. If one is interested in looking at history right from the beginning, the whole foundation of humanity is built on the idea that those who are not with us are against us. That's what is operating in human thinking. So, to kill and to be killed in the name of God, represented by the church in the West, and all the other religious thinking here in the East, was the order of the day. That's why there is this fundamentalism here in this country now. The Chinese - what horrors they have committed; you will be surprised – they killed scholars and religious people. They burned and buried the books of Confucius and other teachers. Today the political ideologies represented by the state are responsible for the killing of people. And they claim that what they are doing is the result of some great revolution that they had started. Revolution is nothing but the revaluation of our values. It does not mean anything. After a while it settles down.

By nature I mean the whole thing that is there. The life forms around – the assemblage of life around this planet. You are not different from all that. It may not have any purpose at all. What I see is what is happening here and now. But you want to establish a cause-and-effect relationship between the two events. That is the way logical thinking functions in us. Logic is used by us to win an argument over somebody. That also is a destructive weapon; and when logic fails, there is violence. So to ask the question, 'Where have we failed? Why have we taken this wrong turn?' to me has no meaning. But an important question that we have to ask is something else, 'Are there any answers? Are there any solutions for our problems?'

The body does not want to learn anything or know anything, because it has that intelligence – native, innate intelligence – that helps it to survive. If this body is in a jungle, it will survive; if it doesn't, it's gone. But it will fight to the last. That's just the way the human body is functioning. If there is some danger to it, the body throws in everything that is available and tries to protect itself. If it cannot, it gives in. But in a way the body has no death. The atoms in it are put together and what happens at death is a reshuffling of the atoms. They will be used somewhere else. So the body has no birth or death, because it has no way of experiencing that it is alive or that it will be dead tomorrow.

You call this a table, and that you call a dead corpse: but actually there is life there. You see the decomposition that is taking place in the dead body is a form of life. Of course, that's no consolation to the one who has lost his wife. Please don't get me wrong. When death has provided the basis for the continuity of life, how can you call it death? It's a different matter that it is no consolation to me or to the one who has lost his near and dear one. But you can't say that it [the corpse] is dead. Now they are saying that the hair keeps growing, the nails keep growing, and brain waves continue for a long time even after the so-called clinical death.

That is the reason why now they are trying to define death in the courts – there in France and other countries. They find it so difficult to define death. And now in the United States they have gone one step further. They keep the dead bodies in deep freezers so that one day medical science will come up with a cure for the disease that was responsible for the death of that body. Do you know what they will do? They are not going to leave their money to their children. The money will be blocked and it is going to create a tremendous economic stagnation of the movement of money. It's very strange. They call that cryonics.

Where do you draw the line between life and death? The definition of death is eluding the legal profession; so far they are unable to define what death is. For all practical purposes we have to consider that it's the same as clinical death. But in nature there is no birth and there is no death. Nothing is ever born, and nothing ever dies. So, if that [idea] is applied to the body, which is not separate from the totality of life around, there is neither death nor birth for it.

I am not talking metaphysics. We don't seem to understand the basic fact that we are not able to control these things at all. The more we try, the more troubles we are creating… I may sound very cynical, but a cynic really a realist. I am not complimenting myself. I am talking of cynics in general. Cynicism will help you to have a healthy look at the way things are going on in the world.

I don't have any message to give to the world. What I am saying is valid and true for just this moment. That's why people tell me, "You are contradicting yourself all the time". No, not at all. You see, this statement [I am making now] is contradicted by my next statement; a third statement contradicts the first two statements. A fourth statement contradicts rather negates than contradicts the first four, and the fifth one negates the sixth even before it is made! This is done not with the idea of arriving at a positive position; the negation is made for the sake of negation because nothing can be expressed, and you can't say this is the truth. There is no such thing as truth. A logically ascertained premise, yes.

In this particular time frame, all events are independent, and there is no continuity among them. Each event is an independent frame, but you are linking up all these [frames] and trying to channel the movement of life in a particular direction for your ulterior motives. But actually you have no way of controlling the events. They are outside of you. All you can do is establish a relationship with particular events, or put them all together and create a tremendous structure of thought and philosophy.

What Kind Of A Human Being Do You Want?

Our attempts to teach this body, or make it function differently from the way it is programmed by nature, are what are responsible for the battle that is going on.

The moment we ask the question, "Is there something more to our life than what we are doing?" it sets the whole questioning mechanism going. Unfortunately, what has created this interest in Western nations is the so-called Hippy generation. When they tried drugs, the drugs produced a change in what they called their 'level of consciousness'. For the first time they experienced something outside the area of their normal experiencing structure. When once we experience something extraordinary, which actually it is not, we look around for varieties of experiences... More and more of the same. That has created a market for all those people from the Eastern countries, India, China, and Japan, to flood into these countries and promise to provide answers for their questions. But actually they are selling shoddy pieces of goods. What people are interested in are not some answers to their problems but some comforters.

As I said before, they are selling ice packs to numb the pain and make you feel comfortable. Nobody wants to ask the basic question: What is the real problem? What is it that they want? What are they looking for? And this [situation] is taken advantage of by the people from the east. If there is anything to what they claim (that they have the answers and solutions for the problems that we are all facing today), it doesn't seem to be evident in the countries from where they come. The basic question that the Westerners should throw at them is, "Have your answers helped the people of your countries? Do your solutions operate in your own lives?" Nobody is asking them these questions. The hundred different techniques that they offer to you have not been subjected to test. You don't have any statistical evidence to prove that there is something to what they claim. They exploit the gullibility and credulity of the people. When once you have everything that you need, the material goodies, you look around and ask the question, "Is that all there is to it?" And those people exploit that situation. They don't have any answers for the problems facing us today.

What is responsible for the human tragedy or the malady that we are confronted with today is that we are interested in maintaining the identities that are created by our culture. We have tremendous faith in the value system that is created by our culture or society or whatever you want to call it. We never question that. We are only interested in fitting ourselves into that value system. It is that demand from the society or culture to fit us all into that value system that is the cause of man's tragedy.

Somewhere along the line there occurred in human consciousness the demand to find out the answer for loneliness, the isolation that human beings suffer from the rest of the species on this planet. I don't even know if there is any such thing as evolution. If there is, somewhere along the line in that evolutionary process man separated or isolated himself from the rest of the creation on this planet. In that isolation, he felt so frightened that he demanded some answers, some comfort, to fill that loneliness, that isolation from the rest of the life around him. Religious thinking was born out of this situation, and it has gone on for centuries. But it has not really helped us to solve the problems created by mankind. Even the political systems that we have today are nothing but the outgrowth of the spiritual, religious thinking of man. Unfortunately they have failed, and a void has been created. There has been a total failure of our political and economic ideologies.

There is a tremendous danger facing mankind today. The void created by the failure of all these ideologies will be taken advantage of by the religious organizations. They will preach and shout that we all have to go back to the great traditions of our own countries. But what has failed for them is not going to help us to solve our problems.

When some psychologists and scientists came to see me, I made this very clear to them, "You have come to the end of your tether. If you want answers for your problems, you have to find them within your own framework and not look elsewhere, especially the ancient dead cultures of the past". Going back or looking back to those systems and techniques that have failed us is only going to put us on a wrong track, on a merry-go-round.

The situation that we are facing today is only the result of the past, and if we are looking back to the past, we are already dead. We have no future at all as long as we try to get the answers from the past that is dead. Anybody who says, "Look back or go back", has no answers to offer us. The future is blocked if someone tells us, "You have to look back", because it is the past that has put us in the present awkward situation. But we are not ready to brush the whole thing aside.

All the techniques, the ancient techniques of meditation, Yoga, Tantra, Zen Buddhism, Catholicism have totally failed. Otherwise we wouldn't be where we are today. If there were anything to their claims, we would have created a better and happier world. But we are not ready to accept the fact that it is they that are responsible for creating the sorry mess that we are all facing today.

If you look at the political systems like fascism or communism they are very much like a religion. They have their own Church, their own Bible and... Even our procurators have left the church. They have had the big temples accepted the same hierarchies as in the church of the Middle Ages, but all of them have crumbled and still there are millions of victims. We are partly responsible for this situation because we want to be victimized by them. What is the point in blaming those people? There is no point in blaming ourselves either because it is a two-way game: we play the game and they play the game. And playing games is all that we are doing. We are used to patting our own backs and telling ourselves, "God is in the far heavens and all is right with the world". It is very comforting to believe that we are going to do something extraordinary in the future. What we are left with is the hope; and we live in hope and die in hope. What I say doesn't sound promising, but it's a fact.

We keep hoping - that's a very comforting thing - to hope that the future is going to be a marvellous thing and tremendously different from what it has been all these years. But we are not doing anything to create something new.

It is just a rehash of the past, the dead past. We only give new names and put new labels. But basically and essentially it [the religious teaching] has not helped us and it is not going to help us. It is not a question of replacing our ideas with new ideas, our thoughts with new thoughts, our beliefs with new beliefs, for the whole belief structure is very important to us. We do not want to free ourselves from this illusion. If we free ourselves from one illusion, we always replace it with another. If we brush aside or drop one belief, we will always replace that belief with another belief – immediately.

The fact is that we don't want to be free. What is responsible for our problems is the fear of losing what we have and what we know. All these therapies, all these techniques, religious or otherwise, are only perpetuating the agony of man. It is very comforting for people to believe that somehow, through some miracle, they are going to be freed from the problems that they are confronted with today. There is no way out of this because we are all wholly and solely responsible for the problems that we have created for ourselves and for others.

If we have created the problems, we are also fighting them. But we are not ready to accept the fact that what has created the problems cannot itself solve them. What we are using to solve our problems is what we call 'thought'. But thought is a protective mechanism. Thought is only interested in maintaining the status quo. We may talk of change, but when actually the time comes for us to change things, we are not ready for it. We insist that change must always be for the better and not for the worse. We have a tremendous faith in the mechanism that has created the problems for us. After all, that is the only instrument that we have at our disposal, and we don't have any other instrument. But actually it cannot help us at all. It can only create problems, but cannot solve them. We are not ready to accept this fact because accepting it will knock out the whole foundation of human culture. We want to replace one system with another. But the whole structure of culture is pushing us in the direction of completely annihilating all that we have built with tremendous care.

We don't want to be free from fear. Anything you do to free yourself from fear is what is perpetuating the fear. Is there any way we can be freed from fear? Fear is something that cannot be handled by thought; it is something living. So we want to put on our gloves and try to touch it, play with it. All that we want to do is to play games with it and talk about freeing ourselves from fear. Or go to this therapist or that, or follow this technique or that. But in that process, what we are actually doing is strengthening and fortifying the very thing that we are trying to be free from, that is, fear.

If the tremendous amount of energy that we put into solving this problem is released - I say, 'if' - if it is released, what is it that you cannot do? But there is no way you can do anything about it. If you were lucky enough to find yourself in the situation where you are freed from this [fear] and that energy is released, living in this world would be very simple and easy.

So we live in a society based on fear. Even our institutions - police, banks, doctors, insurance, and everything we have created are based on fear. Yes, fear. But what is the point in telling ourselves that we are going to be freed from fear? If that fear comes to an end, you will drop dead, physically! Clinical death will take place! Of course, you and your fear are not two different things. It is comforting to believe that you and fear are not two different things. You are frightened of certain things, or you do not want this or that thing to happen. You want to be free from fear. All this is very comforting, but there is no way you can separate yourself from fear and do anything to free yourself from it. If the fear comes to an end, 'you' as you know yourself, 'you' as you experience yourself, are going to come to an end, and you are not ready for that sort of thing.

The plain fact is that if you don't have a problem, you create one. If you don't have a problem, you don't feel that you are living. So the solutions that we have been offered by the teachers, in whom we have tremendous faith; are not really the solutions. If they were the solutions, the problems wouldn't be there at all. If there were no solutions for the problems, even then the problems wouldn't be there. We would like to live with those problems, and if we are free from one problem, we create another.

Without problems you would be bored, you feel. Boredom is a bottomless pit. There is no way you can be freed from boredom. You love your boredom, but all the time you are trying to free yourself from boredom. As long as you think that there is something more interesting, more purposeful, more meaningful to do than what you are actually doing, you have no way of freeing yourself from boredom. So, it goes on and on. If you don't entertain yourself with a cowboy movie, you might go to a church and pray, or you might go to a temple and pray, or you might want to listen to a holy man telling you all kinds of stories. He will sell you some shoddy piece of goods, "Stand on your head, stand on your shoulders, do this and do that," and you will be all right.

But the basic question which none of us is willing to ask is: what is it that we want? Whether you are in Holland, in America, or in Africa, anywhere, what you are really interested in is the quest for permanent happiness. That is all that we are interested in. all these religious people, the gurus, and the holy men, who are marketing these shoddy pieces of spiritual goods, are telling us that there is some way you can have eternal and permanent happiness. But that doesn't happen. We invest our faith in them so that it gives us hope, and we go on doing the same thing over and over again. And we continue to live in that hope. But it does not help us to get what we are really interested in, namely, to be permanently happy. There is no such thing as permanence at all, let alone permanent happiness.

The quest for permanent happiness is a lost battle; but we are not ready to accept that fact. What we are left with is some moments of happiness and some moments of unhappiness. If we are not ready to accept that situation, and still demand a non-existent permanent happiness, we are not going to succeed.

It is just a question of succeeding, or wanting to be in a permanent state of happiness, but that demand is the enemy of this living organism. The organism is not interested in happiness at all. It is only interested in its survival. What are necessary for the survival of this living organism are its sensory perceptions along with the sensitivity of the senses and nervous system. The moment you find yourself in a happy situation and tell yourself that you are happy; the demand that this happiness should continue for a longer time is bound to be there. And the more you try to prolong that sensation of happiness beyond its natural duration, the more there is danger for this system which is only interested in maintaining its sensitivity. So, there is a battle going on between your demand for permanent happiness and the demand of the body to maintain its sensitivity. You are not going to win this battle; yet you are not ready to give it up.

When you do meditation, you put your body to unnecessary torture. The body suffers. It is not interested in your techniques of meditation, which actually are destroying the peace that is already there. It is an extraordinarily peaceful organism. It does not have to do anything to be in a peaceful state. By introducing this idea of a peaceful mind, we set in motion a sort of battle, and the battle goes on and on. But what you feel, what you experience as the peaceful state of mind, is a war-weary state of mind, you want more and more of the same. This creates problems for the body. And by wanting more of the same, you literally harm the body. And you pay a heavy price.

When a baby cries, it has no idea of crying. If you let the baby cry it will eventually stop. Automatically. The baby will be exhausted. The baby cries because it is trying to express through that crying some discomfort. But we don't understand what the discomfort is. We are interested only in our comfort, and that is why we try to stop the baby from crying. We have created a neurotic situation for the baby from the very start. We don't have the energy to deal with the problems of living beings, and the child is a living thing. It would be more interesting to learn from children, than try to teach them how to behave, how to live and how to function.

Because we suppress everything in us, we want to suppress everything in the growing child. We have already created a problem for the child instead of finding out what actually is his problem. We don't have the energy to deal with the problems of children. We curse them and then we push them to fit into this framework of ours, created by us for our own reasons.

This is what we call culture. Culture is not anything mysterious. It is your way of life and your way of thinking. All the other cultural activities we consider to be very creative are part and parcel of your way of living and thinking. And your way of thinking is the thing that has created all these problems for you. There is no way you can free yourself from the problems created by thinking except by setting in motion another kind of thinking. But that cannot be of help.

Actually there are no thoughts there [within you]. Thoughts are not self-generated. They are not spontaneous. We never look at a thought. What is there is about thought but not thought itself. We are ready to question that and face the fact that thoughts are not spontaneous. They come from outside in the sense that when there is a sensory response to a stimulus, we translate that sensation within the framework of our knowledge, and tell ourselves that that [the translation] is the sensation. You recognize the sensation and give a name to it. That is what memory is all about. What is there is only memory. Where is that memory? Really, nobody knows where memory is. You can say that it is in the neurons. When once the sensory perceptions activate the senses that are involved, they in their turn, activate the memory cells. We capture every movement there [in the sensation] within the framework of the memory structure and translate it.

Naturally, memory is born out of our demand to isolate ourselves, censor the sensory perceptions and filter them in order to maintain the status quo and continuity of the movement of our knowledge. We may talk of freeing ourselves from knowledge. But whatever we are doing is not freeing us from the movement of knowledge. On the contrary, it is strengthening and fortifying the very thing that we are trying to be free from.

We are creating the universe ourselves. We have no way of looking at the universe at all. The model that we see is created by our thought. Even the scientists who say that they are observing certain things have actually no way of observing anything except through the mirror of their own thinking. The scientist is influencing what you are looking at. Whatever theories he comes up with are only theories; they are not facts to him. Even if you are looking at the object physically, without the interference of thought and without translating what you are looking at, the physical looking is affecting the object that you are looking at. Actually there is no way you can capture, contain and give expression to what you are looking at. You dare not look at anything. Scientists can come up with all kinds of theories, hundreds and hundreds of them. You can only reward them with Nobel prizes or give them some prestigious awards, and that is all that they are interested in. But, are we ready to accept the fact that there is no way that you can look at anything? You are not looking at anything at all. Even the physical looking is influenced by your thought. There is no way you can look at anything without the use of the knowledge that you have of what you are looking at. In fact, it is that [the knowledge] that is creating the object. It is your thinking that is creating the observer. So this whole talk of the observer and the observed is balderdash. There is neither the 'observer' nor the 'observed'. [The talk of] the 'perceiver' and the 'perceived', the 'seer' and the 'seen' is all bosh and nonsense. These themes are good for endless metaphysical discussions. There is no end to such discussions. And to believe that there is an observation without the observer is a lot of baloney. There is no way you can look at anything without the 'looker', who is the product of this thinking.

Important scientists from all over the world from different disciplines, people from the spiritual world and the world of industry and economics, have come together to talk about the similarities among their respective disciplines instead of differences. All of them seem to feel that they should support each other.

I feel, the scientists, by looking or asking for help from religious people, are committing the biggest of all blunders. They have come to the end of their tether. If they have problems in their systems, they have to solve them by and for themselves. The religious people have no answers for the problems created by the scientific thinking of man. I do not know if by coming together and exchanging their views or giving speeches they are going to achieve anything. I may sound very cynical when I say that nothing is going to come out of it except that they will make speeches and feel comfortable that they are trying to understand each other's point of view. When you say something to someone, he will say that that is your point of view. But he does not realize that his also is a point of view. So, how can there be any communication between two people who have different points of view? The whole purpose of the conversation or dialogue is only to convert the other man to your point of view. If you have no point of view, there is no way he can convince or convert you to his point of view. So this dialogue is between two points of view and there is no way you can reconcile them.

It would be something like the United Nations. (The United Nations is the biggest joke of this century. If each one is trying to assert his own rights there, how can there be a United Nations?) The problem is that thought creates frontiers everywhere. Differences. That's all it can do.

So it is thought that has created the world; and you draw lines on this planet, "This is my country, that is your country". So, how can there be unity between two countries? The very thing that is creating the frontiers and differences cannot be the means to bridge the different viewpoints. It is an exercise in futility. I may sound very cynical when I point this out. But they know in their hearts that nothing will come out [of their deliberations]. We are not ready to accept the fact that thought can only create problems. That instrument cannot be of any help to us.

The talk of intuition and insight is another illusion. Every insight you have is born out of your thinking. The insights strengthen and fortify the very thing you are trying to be free from. All insights, however extraordinary they may be, are worthless. You can create a tremendous structure of thought from your own discovery, which you call insight. But that insight is nothing but the result of your own thinking, the permutations and combinations of thought. Actually there is no way you can come up with anything original there. There is no thought that you can call your own. I don't have any thoughts which I call my own - not one thought, not one word, not one experience. Everything comes from outside. If I have to experience anything, I have to depend upon the knowledge that is put in here. Otherwise there is no way you can experience anything. What you do not know, you cannot experience. There is no such thing as a new experience at all.

I even question the idea of consciousness. They may not be any such thing as consciousness at all, let alone the subconscious, the unconscious, and all the other levels of consciousness. How do you become conscious of a thing? You become conscious of a thing only through your memory. First, you recognize it. And the recognition and naming are all that are there. You can trick yourself into the belief that recognition and naming are two different things. But actually they are not. The very fact that you recognize something as an object even without naming it means that you already know about it. The memory that has captured it says that it is an object. The talk about recognition without naming is a very clever way of playing a game. It is only sharpening your intellect. Actually you are not trying to understand what the problem is or how to deal with it.

Instinct is another idea invented by thought. Whatever we experience is thought-induced. What you don't know you cannot experience. To experience a thing, you have to 'know'. For instance, when people from a jungle in Africa were shown their photograph, they could not recognize themselves at all.

The recognition of yourself as an entity is possible only through the help of the knowledge [you have about yourself]. We start this process with children. You tell a child: "Show me your teeth, show me your nose, show me your ears, or tell me your name". That is where identity starts. The constant use of memory to maintain that identity is the situation we find ourselves in. We do not want that identity to come to an end. We do everything possible to maintain it. But the effort to maintain your identity is wearing you out.

The constant use of memory to maintain our identity will put us all ultimately in a state where we are forced to give up. When someone gives up the attempt to fit him or herself into the value system, you call that person crazy. He (or she, as the case may be) has given up. Some people don't want to fit into that framework. We push them to be functional. The more we push them to be functional, the crazier they become. Actually, we are pushing them to suicide.

The alternatives before mankind are either suicide or the fashionable disease, what we call Alzheimer's Disease. Whether the disease occurs due to damaged tissue in the brain or through the use of aluminium vessels, as some claim, they really don't know yet. But this seems to be the fate of mankind. These are the only ways your identity can be destroyed. It is amazing how thousands and thousands of people are affected by it. Even middle-aged people are affected. The constant use of memory to maintain your identity, whether you are asleep, awake or dreaming, is what is going to destroy not only the human species, but also all forms of life on this planet. It is not a happy prophecy. I am not a prophet. I am not prophesying anything. But from what we know and what is happening today, that seems to be the fate of mankind.

Even if we discover the laws of nature, for whatever reason we are interested in doing so, ultimately they are used to destroy everything that nature has created. This propaganda that the planet is in danger is media hype. Everybody has in fact forgotten about it. Actually it is not the planet that is in danger, but we are in danger. We are not ready to face this situation squarely. We must not look for answers in the past or in the great heritage of this or that nation. And we must not look to the religious thinkers. They don't have any answers. If the scientists look to the religious leaders for their solutions, they are committing the biggest blunder. The religious people put us all on the wrong track, and there is no way you can reverse the process.

I am not here to save mankind or prophesy that we are all heading toward a disaster. I am not talking of an Armageddon, nor am I prophesying that there is going to be any paradise on this planet. It is the idea of a paradise, the idea of creating a heaven on this earth, which has turned this beautiful paradise that we already have on this planet into a hell. We are solely responsible for what is happening. And the answers for our problems cannot come from the past and its glory, or from the great religious teachers of mankind. Those teachers will naturally claim that you have failed and that they have the answers for the problems that we are confronted with today. I don't think that they have any answers. We have to find out the answers, if there are any, for ourselves and by ourselves.

'You image is your best friend,' is a sales pitch; it's very interesting. In fact, it's the other way round: the image we have is responsible for our problems. What, after all, is the world? The world is the relationship between two individuals. But that relationship is based on the foundation of, "What do I get out of a relationship?" Mutual gratification is the basis of all relationships. If you don't get what you want out of a relationship, it goes sour. What there is in the place of what you call a 'loving relationship' is hate. When everything fails, we play the last card in the pack, and that is 'love'. But love is fascist in its nature, in its birth, in its expression and in its action. It cannot do us any good. We may talk of love but it doesn't mean anything. The whole music of our age is all around that song, "Love, Love, Love…" You want to assure yourself and assure your friend that you love. Why do you need the assurance all the time that you love the other individual?

There are no questions but only answers. We already have the answers. I don't have any questions of any kind. How come you have questions? The only kind of questions I have are ones like, "How does this microphone work?" I ask that because I don't know its working. I have questions only as to how these mechanical things are operating. For living situations, we have no answers at all. You cannot apply this mechanical, technical know-how, which we have acquired through repeated study, to solve the problems of living.

We are not really interested in solving the latter kind of problems. We do not know a thing about life. Nobody knows. You can only give a definition. What we know is that our living has become terribly boring. We want a way out of that situation. So we have invented all kinds of ways of entertaining ourselves, whether it is the church or politics or entertainment or music or Disneyland. Yet there is no end to that at all. You need more and more. There comes a time when you will not be able to find anything to free yourself from this boredom of life.

I watch television. I turn off the sound and watch the movement only. I like to watch the commercials because most of the commercials are more interesting than the programmes. If people can fall for the commercials, they can fall for anything that these religious people are selling today in the market. How can you fall for those commercials? But they are very interesting. It is not the commercials nor what they are selling that interests me, but the technique of salesmanship. They are amazing and more interesting; I am fascinated by those techniques. I am not influenced by what they are selling. If they had customers like me they would be soon out of business. I don't buy anything they are selling.

So, sales pitch is the main literature in America. I don't know how long they can go on like that. But now others have also copied that. Even in India they have commercials. That's what has happened in Russia as well. It is not your [American] ideas of democracy or freedom that have won the country over to your side. It was Coca Cola, I think, in China, and Pepsi Cola in Russia. Why do you have to sell organically grown potato chips in Russia? I want to know. They have also opened a McDonald's there. That's all that the West can offer to them. That is how it [commercialism] is spreading. If America survives, if we survive, and if we don't destroy ourselves through our own idiotic ways of living and thinking, the American way of life is going to be the way of life. Even in the third world countries including India they have these supermarkets. They are very innovative, the Americans. So, it [commercialism] is spreading all over.

People say that the problem with the supermarkets is that people develop a thieving tendency. I am not against stealing, but I tell people, "Steal but don't get caught". It is stupid to get caught. All the politicians, the whole government machinery thrives on stealing, promising something which they cannot deliver.

It is amazing that we have tremendous faith in all these religious people who cannot deliver the goods. In a business deal, if your partner refuses or fails to deliver the goods, that is the end of the business relationship. But here in the area of religion they can get away with just promising something. They don't deliver the goods at all. How we can fall for that kind of a thing is beyond me. The whole con game has gone on for centuries. But why do we allow ourselves to be conned by those con men? There is not a single exception. All these spiritual teachers of mankind from the very beginning have conned themselves into the belief that they have the answers, the solutions for mankind. They cannot deliver the goods. They only give us hope. As I said at the beginning, we live in hope and die in hope.

The basic question that we all have to ask is: What kind of human being you want in this world? Or where we want to be.

Society is trying to create the human beings. That is what society has done. You and I have been created by the society, solely and wholly to maintain its continuity, its status quo. You have no way of establishing your own individuality. You have to use that [society and all its heritage] to experience yourself as an entity and to function in this world. If you don't accept the reality of the world as it is imposed on us, you will end up in the loony bin. But we have to accept that. The moment we question the reality of what has been imposed on us we are in trouble.

What I am saying is that you have to answer this question for yourself, "What do we want"? This was my problem. I asked myself, "Is there anything I want other than what they wanted me to want? Is there anything I want to think other than what they wanted me to think?" Nobody could help me in this area, and that was my problem. I had no way of finding out an answer. Wanting not to want what the others wanted me to want was also a want. It never occurred to me that this was no different from all the other wants. Somewhere along the line the question somehow disappeared; I don't know how. What I am left with is something that I have no way of experiencing, and no way of communicating or transmitting to anybody.

That is the difficulty I have when I meet people. I have no way of communicating the certainty that occurred in me that there is no way I can understand anything through the instrument which I used for years and years, the instrument being the intellect. It has not helped me to solve any problem. No understanding is possible through that instrument, but that is the most powerful instrument and the only instrument we have. You cannot brush that aside and throw it away. But that is not the instrument, and there is no other instrument. The talk of intuition only puts us on a merry-go-round. It doesn't lead us anywhere.

They say that the 'heart' understands. You are making this assumption that to have a 'heart' is better than to use your head.

The whole religious thinking is built on the foundation of having a good heart and giving supremacy and importance to it, and not to what your 'head' is doing. But what I want to say is that the heart is there only to pump blood. It is not interested in your kindly deeds. If you indulge in kindly deeds, doing good unto others, having a good 'heart', you will only create problems for the heart. It is the beginning of your cardiac problems! That's going to be a real problem. It is your kindly deeds that are responsible for the cardiac arrests and heart failures, and not any [mal] functioning of the heart. The tremendous importance that we have given to the 'heart' is totally irrelevant. To make a distinction between the 'head' and the 'heart' is interesting, but in the long run it is not going to help us.

The reality of the matter is that even your feelings are thoughts. If you tell yourself that you are happy, you are translating that sensation of happiness within the framework of the knowledge you have. So that too is a thought. There are no pure feelings at all. What you are stuck with are only thoughts, and those thoughts are put in there by your culture.

We have also invented this idea of freeing yourself from thoughts. How are you going to succeed in freeing yourself from thoughts? It is only through the help of another thought. Actually there are no thoughts there at all. What you find there is that the very question that we ask ourselves and ask others, namely, "Is there a thought?", is itself born out of thought. If you want to look at thought and find out for yourself if there is any such thing as thought, what you will find there is [a thought] about thought but not thought itself. So we really don't know if there are any thoughts, let alone good thoughts or bad thoughts. And there is no thinker there either. The thinker, the non-existent thinker, comes into being only when you use your thought to achieve your goals. It doesn't matter what the goal is, or whether it is material or spiritual. When once you use thoughts to achieve a goal, we create a non-existent thinker. But actually there is no thinker. There is nobody who is talking now. There is only 'talking', there is only 'seeing', there is only 'listening'. But the moment you translate that listening, interpret it in terms of the framework of your reference point; you have created a problem. Its [thought's] interest is to interpret and translate. It helps only to strengthen and fortify the very thing, which you are trying to free yourself from.

It is like a dog chasing its own tail; or like you're trying to overcome your own shadow. Your wanting to over-take your own shadow is an exercise in futility.

Because money is the most important factor in our lives, they say that money is the root cause of all evil. But actually, it is not the root cause of evil; it is the root cause of our existence, of our survival. I sometimes say that if you worship that god, the money god, you will be amply rewarded. If you worship the other God, whether he exists or not is anybody's guess, you will be stripped of everything you have, and he will leave you naked in the streets. It is better to worship the money god. And you will be amply rewarded. Tell me one person who is not thinking of money. Not one person on this planet. Even the holy ones who talk about their indifference to money are concerned about it. How do you think they will get ninety-two Rolls Royces? You try and buy one Rolls Royce car; you will know how difficult it is. For the religious people it is easy because other people deny themselves and give their money to them. So you can be rich at another man's expense. How much money you need is a different matter. Each one has to draw his own line. But when once your goals and needs are the same, then the problem is very simple.

The goals and needs are the same. You have no goals beyond your needs or beyond your means.

When once that becomes a reality in your life, it becomes very simple to live in this world, the complex and complicated world created by us all. We are responsible for this world. When once this demand to change yourself into something better, something other than what you actually are, is not there, the demand to change the world also comes to an end. I don't see anything wrong with the world. What is wrong with this world? The world can't be anything different from what we are. If there is a war going on within us, we cannot accept a peaceful world around us. We will certainly create war. You may say that it all depends upon who is responsible for the war. It is simply a point of view as to who is calling another a warmonger and oneself the 'peace-monger'. The peace-mongers and the warmongers sail in the same boat. It is something like the pot calling the kettle black, or the other way around: the kettle calling the pot black.

These old proverbs are quite to the point. They are really the utterances of wise men who have observed the reality of the world exactly the way it is.

There is nothing to understand. How that understanding dawned on me, I really don't know. The understanding that this instrument [the intellect] is really not the instrument to understand anything is something that cannot be communicated. This instrument is only interested in perpetuating itself through what it calls 'understanding', which in reality is its own machination. It is only sharpening itself to maintain its own continuity. When once you know that it is the instrument and that there is no other instrument, then there is nothing more to understand.

It is actually quite simple. But this very simple fact of our life, of our existence, is something, which the complex structure that we have created is not ready to accept, because its very simplicity is going to shatter the complexity. What, after all, is evolution, if there is any such thing as evolution? It is the simple becoming complex. The complex structure is not ready to face this situation - the very simplicity of the whole process. When once that is understood, the whole theory of evolution collapses. Maybe there is such a thing as evolution. We really don't know for sure. When once you accept that there is an evolution in the life around, you put the same thing in the spiritual realm and say that there is also spiritual progress. You will say, "I am more evolved than my neighbour, spiritually speaking, and more evolved than my fellow beings". That makes us feel superior to all.

I am more spiritual than my fellow beings... So the very complexity, which we are responsible for, is not ready to leave that simple thing alone, to leave it simple.

It is a very misleading phrase, to accept 'what is'. It is very interesting to talk about 'what is', but you cannot describe that 'what is' in any manner. And you cannot leave 'what is' as it is. You cannot even complete the sentence and say, 'what is is'. But we don't stop there. We build a tremendous structure, the fantasy structure, romantic structure, on 'what is' and talk about love, bliss, beatitude, or immensity.

We dare not leave that 'what is' alone. It implies that you are still grappling with what you romantically phrase as 'what is'. It is like dealing with the unknown. There is no such thing as the unknown. The known is still trying to make the unknown part of the known. It is a game that we play. That is how we fool ourselves in our approach to problems. All our positive approaches have failed. And we have invented what is called the 'negative approach'. But the negative approach is still interested in the same goal that the positive approach is interested in. What is necessary for us is to free ourselves from the goal. When once we are freed from the goal [of solving problems], the question of whether it is a positive approach or a negative approach does not even arise.

In nature the positive and the negative don't exist at all. If they do, they exist in the same frame. That is what these scientists are talking about. If you observe the universe, there is chaos in it. The moment you say there is chaos; in the same frame, there is also order. So, you cannot, for sure, say that there is order or chaos in the universe. Both of them are occurring simultaneously.

That is the way the living organism also operates. The moment thought is born; it cannot stay there. Thought is matter. When once the matter that is necessary for the survival of the living organism is created, that matter becomes part of energy. Similarly, life and death are simultaneous processes. It is thought that has separated and created the two points of birth and death. Thought has created this space and this time. But actually, birth and death are simultaneous processes.

You cannot say whether you are born or dead. You cannot say that you are alive or dead. But if you ask me the question, "Are you alive?" I would certainly say, "I am alive". So my answer is the common knowledge you and I have about how a living being functions. That is how I say that I am a living being and not a dead person. But we give tremendous importance to these ideas. We sit and discuss them everlastingly and produce a tremendous structure of thought around them.

So, what kind of human being do you want? Culture, society, or whatever you want to call it, has placed before us the model of a perfect being, which is the model of the great spiritual teachers of mankind. But it is not possible for every one of us to be like that. You are unique in your own way. There is no way you can copy those men. That is where we have created the tremendous problem for the whole of mankind.

People want to be like the Buddha... or like Jesus. Thank God, you cannot be like Jesus because there is one and only one Jesus. To that extent many people are saved from trying to be like Jesus. But in India they accept Jesus also as one of the great teachers of mankind. They tell themselves and others that Jesus is there to enable you to become a Christ and not a Christian. But that is not acceptable by the Christians, because it destroys the whole foundation of the church; it destroys the whole foundation of Christianity. If there was a Christ, you have to accept his word when he says, "I am the way, I am the truth, and I am the life.

Through me you will reach the eternal Father". That statement, whether he made it or someone else put it in his mouth, has created the foundation for the whole church. You cannot exonerate the leaders of the church and only blame the followers for the sorry mess of things they have created for us.

The whole ethical culture and everything that we have created to rule ourselves with are born out of the thinking of man. We are not ready to accept the fact that nature probably is interested in creating only perfect species and not perfect individuals. Nature does not use any model. It creates something; then it destroys it, and creates something else. The comparative process characteristic of thinking seems to be absent.

So what kind of human being do you want? The whole ethical culture that is built by us to shape the actions of man has totally failed. The commandment, "Thou shall not steal", has not helped. If you want to free a human being from thieving tendencies, we have to find some other way of doing it, whatever your reasons are to free him from those tendencies. Probably you have to find a drug to change the chemistry of those who have the tendencies.

But there is also a danger, a tremendous danger. When once you perfect genetic engineering and transform human beings through chemical means or genetic engineering, you will certainly hand the means over to the state. Then it becomes easy for the state to control people without brainwashing them. Brainwashing takes decades and decades, probably even centuries. The fact that we have outlawed murder has not put an end to murder. It's only on the increase. I am not for a moment saying that if murder is not outlawed, there will be fewer murders. In spite of outlawing murder, murder is on the increase. Why is that so? Your argument will be that if it is not outlawed, there will be more murders. But I am not impressed by that logic at all. Why is murder on the increase?

The moment you condemn certain things; people have ways and means of overcoming them....

When we are against something or trying to get rid of something, it will keep growing. We are not ready to accept that. Whatever we are doing to free ourselves from the problems that we have created is what is perpetuating them.

The body is not interested in your perceptions. It is not interested in learning anything from you or knowing anything from you. All the intelligence that is necessary for this living organism is already there. Our attempts to teach this body, or make it function differently from the way it is programmed by nature, are what are responsible for the battle that is going on. There is a battle between what is put in by culture and what is inherent there in the body.

The body knows what is good for itself. It can survive and it has survived for millions of years. It is not concerned about your pollution or your ecology, or about the way you are treating it. What it is concerned with is in its own survival. And it will survive. There is no doubt about it. When the time comes, it will probably flush the whole thing [the cultural input] out of its system. That would be the luckiest day for mankind. That is something that cannot be achieved through any volition or effort, or through the help of any teacher who says that there are ways and means of freeing you from the stranglehold of your thoughts.

There is no way out. The solution for your problems is to accept the fact that there is no way out. And out of that [acceptance] something can come. Anything you do to get out of this trap, which you yourself have created, is strengthening and fortifying it.

You are not ready to accept the fact that you have to give up. A complete total surrender. I don't want to use that word 'surrender', because it has certain mystical overtones. It is a state of hopelessness, which says that there is no way out of this situation. Any movement, in any direction, on any level, is taking you away from that. Maybe something can happen there, we don't know. But even that hope that something will happen is still a hope.

Do we give up then? You see, giving up something in the hope of getting something else in its place is not really giving up. There is nothing to give up there. The very idea of giving up, the very idea of denying certain things to yourself, is in the hope of getting something else.

Sometimes it so happens that when you give up everything without any expectations the problem gets automatically resolved. This happens to all those who are working out some mathematical or scientific problem. They go to sleep when they are exhausted, and that gives some time for the mechanism that is involved, and you are ready with the answer. It is not some miraculous thing. You give some time for the computer to work out a solution to your problem. On its own it comes out with the answer, but only if there is an answer. If there is no answer then that is the end of the story.

So basically this means you can't do a thing; yet you don't stop there. All those who say that you can do something are telling you that there is a way out. Yet you can't sit down without doing anything.

You cannot stop the movement of life. It goes on… You don't try to channel the movement of life in any particular direction to produce any special results. So you let go.

Our language structure is such that there is no way you can be free from a dualistic approach to problems. I don't want to use the word 'dualistic' because it again has religious connotations.

There is nothing beyond words. Memory is playing a trick with itself because it tells you that it is not the words that you are left with but something other than the words. But the fact that you remember something of what has gone on between us both implies that the impact of the words is translated by memory, which then tells you that it [the memory] is something other than the words.

Thoughts are outside the field of the body. I don't think that the brain has anything to do with creativity at all. The brain is just a reactor and a container.

What is memory after all? Nobody knows what it is. You can give a definition as a student of psychology. "Memory is the mental response of recalling a specific thing at a specific time". That was the definition that I had learned in psychology textbooks. But that is too silly a definition because nobody knows what memory is or where it is located. You can examine the brain after you are dead, after I am dead. But you won't see any difference between the brain of a genius and the brain of a low-grade moron. So we really don't know. A scientist comes out with some theory. You may award him a Nobel Prize. Then someone else comes along, blasts his theory and offers another one. Every leap year there is a new theory.

There is also this talk about the morphogenetic field. That implies that there is something that you can do with the genes. The whole motivation, if I may use that word, behind all this is that you still want to do something, change something. All the research projects are geared to the idea of learning something about the way memory operates and the way the human body is functioning, so that you can then apply what you have discovered, which is very limited in the first place. It [the subject matter of life, the human body, and memory] is such a vast thing that what you know is only a teeny-weeny bit of what there is. Your only interest is to bring about a change. But we are not ready to accept that there is nothing to be changed. Scientific discoveries are microscopic compared to the destructive use we put them to. What we have discovered of the laws of nature is only used for destructive purposes. We have tremendous weapons of destruction today. If the church has these instruments of destruction, I don't think you and I would be here, much less evolve any other way of dealing with our problems and our lives.

The Russian Orthodox Church will have another heyday. That's all right, but all these countries from East to West, North to South, will step in now. I am glad that there are more enlightened people in the West than in India. The Westerners are not talking of just their Christianity. They claim that they are enlightened people, and they are out to enlighten the vast millions. Maybe one of these days all these people will go to India and try to enlighten the people there.

It's good in a way because that will put an end to all those teachers coming from the Eastern countries to exploit the people here in the West. It would be interesting if you import all that religious stuff into these countries and give your high-tech and technology to those third world countries. They will most probably be able to compete with you in the West.

I don't live in any particular place. I am here today, and tomorrow I will be in America, or God knows where. I have no fixed abode. I have no tangible means of livelihood. That is the definition of a vagabond. Mine is a sort of gypsy life. I have just enough money to travel and take care of my physical needs. So, I don't depend upon anyone. The world does not owe a living to me. Why should the world feed me? I am not contributing anything to the world. Why should the world feed me and take care of me?

I don't want many people. I am trying to avoid all the seekers. Here they have invented the word 'finders'. 'Finders' means those who have found the truth. I don't want seekers. And if there are any finders, they don't need my help. By allowing myself to be surrounded by those people, I am inadvertently participating in the illusion that by carrying on a dialogue or a conversation with me they are getting something.

So lately I have been discouraging people. Even if they just come and sit around me, I try to point out the ridiculous nature of this get together. I try to finish it by saying, "Nice meeting you all". But still they don't go. They would sit with me for hours and hours. Even if I get up and go away, they would be still there sitting and talking. They would be talking about what I did or did not say, or what they thought I had said. It's happening everywhere and in India too. But there we are used to this kind of thing.

I have been very emphatic these days saying that I don't want to see Krishnamurti's 'widows'. Most of those who come to see me are the followers of J. Krishnamurti. I mean J. Krishnamurti freaks, and also the 'widows' of Rajneesh, and all kind of religious buffs - of all shapes, sizes, and colours. Unless they have some sort of background in all this, they can't be interested in this kind of thing. They come to receive some confirmation from me about what they are interested in. But they find that they are not getting anything from me. Still they continue to come. You have no idea of how many thousands and thousands of people have passed through the precincts of my homes in India, America, Europe, Australia, and New Zealand. Some of them are intelligent enough to realize that they are not going to get anything from me and that there is no point in hanging around me. But still I have a few friends, whom I call my Enemies Number One, Two, Three, Four, Five etc. They hang around me, but I don't think they expect anything from me. I am not so sure that they don't expect anything from me. They are not ready to accept what I emphasize and assert all the time: that whatever has happened to me has happened despite everything I did. Some friends who have been with me for years say that they still have the hope that they are going to get something from me. This, in short, is the story of my life.

If you try to destroy the authority of others, you in your own way become the authority for others. How to avoid that [becoming an authority] is really a problem for me. But in some sense it's not really a problem.

I cannot accept seekers because it is very clear to me that I cannot be of any help to them, and that they don't need any help from me. What they are interested in they can get somewhere else. There are so many people who are selling in the marketplace. They are interested in selling comforters. That is where these people should go, and not hang around me.

The whole thought of religious thought is built on the foundation of discipline. Discipline to me means a sort of masochism. We are all masochists. We torture ourselves because we think that suffering is a means to achieve our spiritual goals. That's unfortunate.

Life is difficult. So discipline sounds very attractive to people. With great honour we say, "He has suffered a lot". We admire those who have suffered a lot to achieve their goals. As a matter of fact, the whole religious thinking is built on the foundation of suffering. If not for religion, you suffer for the cause of your country in the name of patriotism...

Those who impose that kind of discipline on us are sadists. But unfortunately we are all being masochists in accepting that. We torture ourselves in the hope of achieving something...we are slaves of our ideas and beliefs. We are not ready to throw them out. If we succeed in throwing them out, we replace them with another set of beliefs, another body of discipline. Those who are marching into the battlefield and are ready to be killed today in the name of democracy, in the name of freedom, in the name of communism, are no different from those who threw themselves to the lions in the arenas. The Romans watched that fun with great joy. How are we different from them? Not a bit. We love it. To kill and to be killed is the foundation of our culture.